Praise for *Transcending High-Conflict Divorce:*

"Based on Virginia Gilbert's extensive clinical experience, this gem of a book will help readers detach from a high-conflict ex and learn tools to feel empowered rather than stuck in the past. I strongly recommend this reader-friendly book to parents who are going through a high-conflict divorce and want to get over their ex, focus on what they can control, and put their children first."
—Terry Gaspard, author of *Daughters of Divorce* and owner of MovingPastDivorce.com

"If you're struggling with a high-conflict ex, this is the book you've been waiting for. Put away the psychology volumes describing the various personality disorders. Here, Virginia Gilbert gives you that information and more as she breaks down the dynamics of a high-conflict divorce, offers understanding (she's been there too), and then (the best part) delivers specific tools to empower you. The title doesn't lie: These pages aren't merely about dealing with a difficult ex, they are about transcending the situation. Read it and free yourself."
—Tara Eisenhard, divorce co:
The D-Word: Divorce Throug┠

D1225504

"I have been a fan of Virginia Gilbert's work for years. She understands high-conflict divorce to a level that is very rare, even amongst her fellow mental health professionals. What I have discovered through my advocacy in the family court system is that the professionals who truly understand this nightmare are the ones who have personally lived it. These are the people that I lean on to navigate the world of high-conflict divorce or child custody battles. If you find yourself in the darkness and are looking to rise above the madness, Virginia Gilbert's new book, *Transcending High-Conflict Divorce,* is the road map to help you reclaim your power."
—Tina Swithin, founder of OneMomsBattle.com and author of *Divorcing a Narcissist*

"An illuminating and practical guide to recovery from a contentious divorce. Therapist Virginia Gilbert explains the addictive nature of anger and conflict. This insightful book teaches how to modify our responses to our adversaries so we may co-parent successfully, gain self-knowledge, and move on with our lives gracefully."
—Rosemary Lombardy, author of *Breaking Bonds: How to Divorce and Abuser and Heal*

TRANSCENDING HIGH-CONFLICT DIVORCE

HOW TO DISENGAGE FROM YOUR EX AND FIND YOUR POWER

Virginia Gilbert, MFT

Transcend Press
LOS ANGELES, CA.

Virginia Gilbert/Transcend Press
7257 Beverly Blvd, Suite 108
Los Angeles, CA. 90036
www.VirginiaGilbertMFT.com

Copy editing and book production Stephanie Gunning
Cover design Gus Yoo
Book Layout ©2019 Book Design Templates

Ordering information: Special discounts are available on quantity purchases by corporations, associations, and others. For details, contact the author at the address above.

Transcending High-conflict Divorce/Virginia Gilbert.
—1st ed.

ISBN 978-0-578-50640-1 (paperback)

To my clients and blog readers:

Your desire to transcend high-conflict divorce inspired this book.

Contents

AUTHOR'S NOTE

The names and identifying details of some of the people mentioned in the book have been changed to protect their privacy. In some cases, the stories are composites of several people's experiences.

Your Roadmap Out of Divorce Hell

"For a long time, divorce was the most important thing about me. Now it's not."[1]

–Nora Ephron

Aren't all divorces high-conflict?

Actually, no. Most divorces follow a natural progression. They start out with conflict that dies down, and eventually become amicable.

A high-conflict divorce doesn't progress. It's relentlessly horrible. Instead of moving on with their lives, the two exes remain psychologically engaged. They don't "get over it," even if one or both remarry and start new families. They aren't able to "put the children first."

Childless couples that can walk away from one another as soon as the division of marital assets has

1

been resolved tend to have easier splits than couples with children whose custody must be negotiated. Having children together forces former spouses to stay related.

High-conflict divorce includes one or more of the following elements.

- Combative electronic correspondence
- Inability to co-parent effectively
- Custody battles
- Poor boundaries, such as trying to run the other parent's house
- Parental alienation—meaning, turning the child against the other parent
- Repeated litigation, often over minor issues
- Extreme emotional reactivity to the other

As a therapist specializing in divorce issues, I've found that high-conflict exes are not really fighting about the things they say they are. *They're fighting because they have a need to blame the other person.* Blame keeps them from completing the developmental task of divorce.

Developmental Task of Divorce? What's That?

Imagine Max, a floundering young adult who blames all his problems on his parents. He's convinced he's not farther along in life because his parents didn't love him enough, didn't love him the right way, got divorced, stayed miserably married, put too much pressure on him, didn't put enough pressure on him, or any number of parental transgressions.

Max is just one of many young adults who have failed to launch. As long as the Maxes of the world keep blaming their parents because they can't hold a job, pay their bills, or maintain a relationship, they won't grow up. They give their power away instead of taking responsibility for their own feelings and choices.

Failure-to-launch divorced people are a lot like this. If they blame their problems and their kids' problems on the ex, or the divorce itself, they'll never create meaningful new lives. Their anger and resentment keep them stuck, effectively married to the person they loathe.

After a while, the fighting and pent-up rage take a toll.

High-conflict Divorce Can Make You Feel Sick

You may be so used to white-knuckling your way through your apocalyptic divorce that you don't realize the impact it's having on your mental and physical health. Take a look at this list. Are you experiencing any of these symptoms?

- Difficulty sleeping and eating
- Crying jags
- Irritability
- Panic attacks (heart palpitations, sweating, difficulty breathing, and thinking you're dying or going crazy).
- Explosive outbursts
- Nightmares
- Isolating
- Difficulty functioning at work
- Feeling overwhelmed with household and child-rearing tasks
- On high alert, waiting for the next disaster
- Hopelessness

While it's normal to feel some of these symptoms at the beginning of divorce, they should not be chronic, especially years after the divorce was initiated.

You don't have to feel this way.

This book is a roadmap out of Divorce Hell. It offers strategies and tools for managing and transcending your high-conflict divorce. I promise, if you follow the steps laid out in the coming chapters—really do the work—your life will improve dramatically.

Why I Wrote This Book

Fifteen years ago, I got divorced. Badly, horribly divorced. My ex-husband and I could agree on nothing. Since we were supposed to co-parent two small children, this was a problem!

Minor issues turned into volcanic eruptions over email. Sometimes we sought counseling together. Sometimes I went on my own. But no therapist knew what to do with us. Many appeared genuinely freaked out by the level of our conflict. I'd leave these counseling sessions feeling scared, frustrated, misunderstood, and ashamed.

Every therapist, every mediator, and every article I read about divorce seemed to preach the same message: No matter how monstrous your situation, if you just do A, B, and C, you can have a successful co-parenting relationship.

The implication was that if you and your ex cannot consciously co-parent, spending warm and fuzzy Thanksgivings together with your kids, you just haven't tried hard enough.

After years of feeling ashamed of being an incompetently divorced person, I stumbled across an internet article on *parallel parenting:* a parenting model for divorced parents who struggle to co-parent. This paradigm advocates that parents limit contact as much as possible. They don't try to coordinate parenting styles. They host separate birthday parties. They avoid being together in front of their children.

Most important, they give up the *fantasy* that they can attain the elusive holy grail of a good divorce.

The idea behind parallel parenting is that *conflict* hurts children, not divorce in and of itself. That limiting parental interaction provides less opportunity for disagreement. And that children would much rather learn to adjust to different sets of rules than to grow up as hostages in a war zone.

Just knowing that there were other divorced people like me made me feel better. I started applying parallel parenting principles to my interactions with my ex. I learned to disengage emotionally. As I practiced these principles—often imperfectly—I started to feel more empowered. It wasn't that the conflict stopped altogether; it was that I changed my relationship to it.

I had learned what I was doing to contribute to the problem and deliberately changed my own behaviors.

Six years ago, I wrote an article for *Huffington Post: Divorce* entitled "What Therapists Don't Tell You about Divorcing a High-conflict Personality." It explained what makes a person high-conflict, and what to do if you have the misfortune of being divorced from one.

People from all over the country who had read the article contacted me seeking my advice. The refrain I heard most often was *"Finally, someone understands my situation."*

I started a private practice specializing in high-conflict divorce. I found that once people hear that they don't have to master the impossible—usually something to do with co-parenting—they stop feeling ashamed. Then they are able to turn their energy to learning strategies to disengage from conflict, manage their reactions, and move on with their lives.

Paradoxically, accepting the reality of a high-conflict divorce sometimes leads to an amicable one. But although I've seen this kind of transformation happen for my clients, as it did in my own life, your focus should not be on making a bad divorce good. *It should be on learning how to detach from the outcome.*

There's Hope!

This book is a blueprint for managing and transcending the conflict in your divorce. It won't do the work for you, but it will give you the tools you need to stop letting divorce run the show and create a life worth living. It is structured in three parts.

In Part One, "What Causes High-conflict Divorce?" you'll learn the anatomy of high-conflict divorce: the types of people that tend to find themselves in one; how divorce drama becomes addictive; and why divorce is an invitation for personal growth.

Part Two, "Strategies for Managing Your High-conflict Divorce," lays out tactics for managing conflict in your divorce. These include effective communication, setting boundaries, parallel parenting, addressing parental alienation, and—extremely important—soothing an overactive nervous system.

Part Three, "Tools for Your Empowerment," gives you a template for personal development. I've modeled some of these tools after steps in Alcoholic Anonymous. As I'll explain in Chapter 6, I believe that high-conflict divorce is like an addiction; just as overcoming a preoccupation with drugs and alcohol requires intense self-examination and behavior modification to change, so does overcoming an addiction to conflict.

If you don't have a spiritual practice, you'll learn why you need one now, and how to establish one (and no, you don't have to believe in God, mantras, or crystals). You'll be taught to use mindfulness skills to modify your relationship to your ex. You'll find tasks here that will help you to identify and change the behaviors that are doing you no good. And you'll be guided to create a design for living that has nothing to do with divorce.

What This Book Is Not

If you're wondering why I haven't mentioned anything about how to win in family court, that's because this book is not a legal guide. There are great books out there that offer advice on how to navigate the family court system, but this isn't one of them.

While it's important to understand legal strategies, *you need to be aware that focusing on litigation actually keeps you emotionally engaged with your ex.*

Some situations demand that you go to court, such as the violation of court orders, to modify custody orders because you or your ex needs to move, or if there is a legitimate safety risk to your children. You *will* learn how to manage the stress of repeated litigation in this book.

Note: This book is not intended as a guide for victims of domestic violence. If you fear that your ex will do you and/or your kids bodily harm, or if he or she has already done so, stop reading and seek protection from a domestic violence shelter, the police, and your attorney. Call the toll-free National Domestic Violence Hotline: 1(800) 799-7233, which is completely anonymous and confidential.

If you have the supreme misfortune of being divorced from a person who thinks of family court as his or her own personal amphitheater, you will have no choice but to go. But most issues don't require a court visit. Too often, litigation does nothing but drain bank accounts and batter psyches. It's crucial to understand that people get answers in family court, but rarely do they get justice.

If you must go to court with a high-conflict spouse, I recommend reading attorney, mediator, and therapist Bill Eddy's books, particularly *Splitting.* Tina Swithin's *Divorcing a Narcissist* is also helpful. (See Recommended Reading).

Keep in mind, though, that no judge can grant you genuine empowerment. Only you can do that. This book will teach you how to shift your focus from things beyond your control to those that are entirely within your control: *your own behaviors and choices.*

If that's something you're ready for, this is the book for you.

PART ONE

WHAT CAUSES HIGH-CONFLICT DIVORCE?

CHAPTER ONE

Mother Teresa Doesn't Marry Hitler . . . or Does She?

There's a saying in family court lore that Mother Teresa never marries Hitler. Meaning: It requires two people of equally pathological behavior to drive high-conflict divorce.

Well, I disagree.

Based on my experience working with people undergoing high-conflict divorces, I can tell you that sometimes Mother Teresa *does* marry Hitler. Sometimes Mister Rogers walks down the aisle with Lady Macbeth.

How Does This Happen?

Perhaps Mother Teresa and Mister Rogers trusted people who weren't trustworthy. Perhaps Hitler and Lady Macbeth used their brains and charm to bamboozle their former spouses. Regardless, it's simplistic to assume that nice people only fall in love with other nice people, or that nasty ones only couple with others of their ilk.

Furthermore, nice people don't always behave perfectly during divorce. Mother Teresa was only human, after all. And Mister Rogers—okay, maybe he was an exception. But most nice people, when pressed hard enough, will lose their cool and do things that make matters worse.

Especially when you're up against an aggressive former spouse who can't tolerate your very existence.

CHAPTER TWO

Personality Disorders
It's All Your Fault!

Peope whose behavior drives apocalyptic divorces are called high-conflict personalities (HCPs). Many of them are *disordered* individuals. Their underlying personality structures and overactive amygdalae—regions in both halves of the brain that experience emotion—cause them to have skewed interpret-ations of reality.

They have features of, or full-blown, personality disorders. Books the size of doorstops have been written about personality disorders that lead to conflict, so I'll do my best to distill that information to the bare essence of what you need to know.

- **Narcissistic personality disorder.** Grandiose and exploitive, narcissists believe they are superior to everyone else.

- **Borderline personality disorder.** Prone to mood swings and having fuzzy identities, borderline people exhibit extreme reactions to any *perceived* abandonment or slight.
- **Histrionic personality disorder.** Seductive and superficial, histrionic people create drama to command the spotlight.
- **Antisocial personality disorder.** The most dangerous of all the personality disorders, antisocial people don't recognize or adhere to social norms. They can't tolerate feeling dominated, so they seek to dominate.
- **Obsessive-compulsive personality disorder.** Slavish devotees of rules so byzantine that only they can understand them, obsessive-compulsives react with outrage and condescension for anyone who veers from their unwritten "handbook."

No matter what flavor of personality disorder your HCP ex-spouse may be, he or she shares key traits with all the others. Bill Eddy, a social worker, lawyer, mediator, and author who is the mastermind behind an organization known as the High-conflict Institute (see Resources), has spent his career analyzing personality disorders that lead to high-conflict divorce. He found that, almost without exception, HCPs exhibit the following qualities.

- **Black-and-white thinking.** HCPs are not nuanced thinkers. They don't see shades of gray. In the mind of your HCP former spouse, he is the good parent and you're the bad parent. He's the brilliant, highly competent poster child for mental health. You, on the other hand, are some version of stupid, crazy, and evil. The HCP's black-and-white thinking also makes him *inflexible;* he doesn't realize that his is not the only way to solve a problem.

- **Emotional reactivity.** Your HCP ex has big feelings that are out of proportion to actual events. She screams at you in front of the children because they told her (when she quizzed them) that you didn't pack edamame in their lunchboxes. She trembles and wipes back tears, with a flourish, as she drops off the kids for a weekend at your house. Whenever you open your mouth during mediation, she practically hyperventilates. She feels entitled to express any feeling, any time, while you, it seems, are not allowed to express any.

- **Extreme behaviors.** Moderation is not in your ex's behavioral toolbox. He storms out of counseling sessions. He ends every email with a threat. He drags you into court to litigate summer camp. He may even be physically violent on occasion.

- **Preoccupation with blame.** Blaming is the hallmark of high-conflict people. Nothing is ever their fault. *You* are to blame for the demise of the marriage, every problem that befalls the children, and any misfortune that may occur, ever, to the end of time. And beyond. Your HCP ex doesn't see her part in problems. (If she did, she'd bump up against guilt, shame, and other feelings she finds intolerable.) *Blaming you serves an important purpose for her; it keeps her from experiencing painful emotions and being accountable for her own actions.*

After reading the blog posts on my website, some people have told me they recognize high-conflict patterns in their own behavior and wonder if *they're* high-conflict people. Are you wondering the same thing? In my experience, most truly disordered individuals lack the self-awareness to assess their personality accurately and have no interest in changing their behavior. They are much too invested in blaming others for their problems. But you might have *features* of disordered thinking and behavior that invite negative reactions from others. If you suspect this is the case, don't panic. In this book, you'll learn techniques for self-improvement.

Aggressive People

George K. Simon, Ph.D., a clinical psychologist who studies highly manipulative individuals, has a slightly different stance on character disordered people. He believes they're inherently *aggressive*. Unlike neurotic people, who feel shame, aggressive people have none. They know what's right, but they don't care. They can't stand the thought of "submitting" to social norms, so they choose to violate them. They don't act out of fear; they act out of a *desire* to take what they want, no matter the cost. When they're denied what they want, they get angry.[1]

Because many highly manipulative people lack a conscience, Simon asserts that therapy, twelve-step programs, and anger management groups won't change them.[2] He urges those who have relationships with this aggressive type to stop hoping they will change.

If you want to know more about managing your interactions with an aggressive ex, Simon's book *In Sheep's Clothing* (see Recommended Reading) offers suggestions.

CHAPTER THREE

Attachment Disorders
Come Here, Go Away

John Bowlby and Mary Main were twentieth-century British psychologists who spent their careers researching how infants and young children bond with their parents. Their joint work, known as *attachment theory,* is now a cornerstone in every mental health professional's graduate program.

Developed from studies of children in wartime, daycare centers, and infant monkeys, attachment theory is complex, as is the actual process of attaching to others. If you want the Ph.D. version, Google away, but in the meantime, here's Attachment 101.

A Secure Base

In order for children to thrive and develop healthy relationship patterns, parents need to provide them with a *secure base.* Feeling secure happens when parents meet their children's needs consistently. They don't have to meet every need every single time (that's impossible), but they have to be nurturing and available *most* of the time.

And by needs, I don't mean "needing" the latest iteration of the iPhone. I'm talking about the essentials: food, shelter, clothing, unconditional love, and emotional attunement (validating and attending to another person's feelings).

Some parents don't, or can't, provide reliable caregiving. They may be abusive and/or suffer from severe mental illness or addiction. They may have a physical condition, like cancer, that keeps them from actively raising their children for a large chunk of time. Other factors, such as moving out during a divorce, can make it difficult for a parent to maintain a stable home environment where they can interact with their children.

A child's early relationship with his caregivers becomes a template for future relationships. If home is a secure base, the child grows up to expect that he will feel loved and safe. If home is a scary, unpredictable place, the child expects more of the same.

The different dynamics that may occur between different children and their caregivers are called *attachment styles.* Interestingly, once established, these styles tend to be consistent across the lifespan. In other words, a child with an anxious attachment style often—but not always—grows up to be an adult with an anxious attachment style.

Here's a closer look.

The Four Adult Attachment Styles

Two of the most common reasons couples come to therapy are a) because they keep having the same arguments, and b) because one person pursues, and the other withdraws. Therapists now recognize that these patterns stem from problems in attachment. Riffing off of Bowlby and Main's studies of childhood attachment, contemporary psychologists are exploring the ways people form connections in adulthood. Here's a breakdown of adult attachment styles.

- **Secure.** People with secure attachment styles had parents they could depend on *most of the time.* They learned how to "do" intimacy. They don't worry about being abandoned. They're comfortable with depending on partners and having partners depend on them.

- **Avoidant**. People with avoidant attachment styles had parents who were aloof, withholding, and demanded self-sufficient children *most of the time.* As adults, they're uncomfortable with closeness. They feel overwhelmed by others' needs. They don't ask for much, and they don't worry about their partners being available to them.
- **Anxious**. People with anxious attachment styles had parents who were inconsistent in their availability *most of the time.* They may have been both intrusive and neglectful. Kids in these circumstances grow up to crave closeness and are terrified of being abandoned. They're *preoccupied* with their relationships, always worrying how things are going. Their clingy behavior and need for constant reassurance can push partners away.
- **Disorganized**. People with disorganized attachment styles generally suffered severe trauma during childhood. Chaos and violence punctuated their home lives. They learned early on that love is dangerous. These individuals tend to repeat the cycle, hurting the people closest to them.

Did you relate to more than one category of attachment style as your own? That's common. Maybe you had one available parent and one not-so available parent. Maybe both parents were lousy, but Grandma was great. Maybe you got therapy to work through your anxious attachment issues and are now feeling pretty secure. Maybe your resilient nature or glass-half-full outlook helped you overcome a less than sunny childhood.

In fact, recent research on attachment suggests that attachment styles are not as fixed as we once thought. Securely attached children can become anxiously attached adults, and anxiously attached kids can become securely attached.

In their book *Attached: The New Science of Adult Attachment and How It Can Help You Find—and Keep—Love*, psychiatrist Amir Levine, M.D., and management consultant Rachel Heller, M.A., write about the role of temperament, neurochemistry, and relationship experiences in our adult attachment styles. They explain that the surest way to change your attachment style for the better is to pick a securely attached partner. Levine and Heller have loads of tips on how to become securely attached in their easy-to-read book.

Although you're not doomed to a life of fractured partnerships simply because your childhood didn't resemble one long series of curated Facebook posts, there *is* a correlation between attachment disorders and awful divorces. Understanding your own attachment issues, as well as those of your ex, can help you to navigate high-conflict divorce.

Problems with Attachment Lead to Personality Disorders

Did you think something seemed familiar when you were reading about attachment styles? If they reminded you of personality disorders, aka character disturbance, you were right! Ruptures in primary relationships during childhood cause trauma. And unresolved trauma often fuels character disturbance: a distorted way of seeing the world and relating to others. Let's take a closer look.

- **Anxious attachment and the borderline personality.** Both are characterized by fear of abandonment, clingy behavior that pushes others away.
- **Avoidant attachment and the narcissistic personality.** Characteristically, such individuals don't like to think about the needs of others.
- **Disorganized attachment and the antisocial personality.** This person hurts others.

What happens when you throw divorce into the mix? Let's consider two scenarios, both featuring a thirty-five-year-old man named Josh.

Scenario 1. An anxiously attached little boy, Josh grows up to be a man with a borderline personality whose chaotic attempts at closeness alienate his securely attached wife, Stella. Despite Stella's efforts to reassure him of her love, Josh is convinced she's cheating on him. In a misguided attempt to manage his abandonment anxiety, he goes out and has an affair. When Stella finds out, she files for divorce. Josh, who's terrified of abandonment, has just gotten himself abandoned all over again! The divorce now triggers his early childhood attachment issues. He becomes frantic in his attempts to get Stella to stay, stalking her, bombarding her with text messages, even threatening to kill himself if she leaves. Concerned about Josh's erratic behavior, Stella files for sole custody of their young son.

One attachment and personality disordered individual plus one securely attached garden-variety individual equals a high-conflict divorce.

Scenario 2. Let's put Josh in a different scenario. Instead of marrying securely attached Stella, he weds an avoidantly attached, narcissist woman named Martha. Josh masks his fear that all women will leave him by having affairs. And because he cheats, he's convinced Martha must be cheating too. This time, his fear that his wife will abandon him is not unfounded; Martha's been unfaithful for years! She exits the marriage with no warning to start a new life with her affair partner. The kicker? She's pregnant. When the baby is born, Josh demands a paternity test. Lo and behold, the infant turns out to be his! Now, not only is his wife leaving him, she's also taking his baby son with her! Martha petitions for full custody on the grounds that her STBX (soon-to-be-ex) is "unfit" and gloats that her new partner will be a better father. Josh tells her he'll never stop fighting for his son, and he'll bleed her dry in the process.

Two attachment and personality disordered individuals equals a really, REALLY high-conflict divorce.

When the Chickens Come Home to Roost

As you can see from the Josh scenarios, a person's unresolved childhood and psychological issues lead to conflict in fraught situations such as divorces that push people's psychological buttons. In both cases, Josh's fear of abandonment and his inability to tolerate genuine intimacy undermined his marriage and exacerbated his divorce.

Did you notice how his divorce from Martha was even worse for Josh than his divorce from Stella? That's because securely attached Stella made choices that were appropriate given the bad circumstances. She didn't inflame things. She didn't file for sole custody of their child to punish Josh; she filed because his behavior indicated that he would not be able to provide a safe home environment.

Avoidantly attached narcissist Martha, on the other hand, wasn't thinking about their baby's needs. She was thinking, as narcissists do, about what was good for Martha. Once she was done with Josh, she tried to obliterate his very existence. She didn't care that he had a right to have a relationship with his child or that her child deserved to know his father. Her attempt to dispose of Josh like yesterday's garbage heightened Josh's abandonment issues. On the surface, yes, Josh was fighting to secure his relationship with his son. But *the way* he was fighting served his unconscious need to stay attached to Martha.

If you're reading this book because you're stuck in a contentious divorce, you're probably hyper-focused on all your STBX's foibles. *That evil narcissist! That crazy borderline! He/she's why we are having such a terrible divorce!*

While your former beloved may be a sorry excuse for a human being, no amount of obsessing about him or her will turn your ex into a decent person. What you *can* change, however, are your own behaviors.

And that begins with recognizing that you, yourself, have a problem.

Ask yourself: "What chickens have come home to roost in my divorce coop? How are my attachment issues replicating themselves in the present?" Consider, for a moment, that you're not reacting to what your ex is or isn't doing. *You're actually reacting (at least in part) to things that happened well before the two of you even met.*

The Hysterical Is Historical

There's a saying in the twelve-step community, which serves people with all different kinds of addictions, from addictions to substances like alcohol and drugs to addictions to processes like gambling and shopping: *The hysterical is historical.* Meaning, when people start acting wacky, they're usually reacting to deep-rooted issues.

Josh cheated on his wife in both the scenarios I concocted, for the same reason—because he had never felt safe growing up. He needed attention and reassurance from more than one woman that he was loved. And because he was terrified to get close, he also cheated to create *distance* from his primary partner.

The come-here/go-away dynamic in his marriage in both scenarios felt familiar to Josh. It was much more tolerable than taking a stand either way: committing to the relationship or leaving altogether. When his wives left him, for very different reasons, his early childhood memories of abandonment resurfaced.

Most people feel destabilized by divorce, but not everyone generates the high drama that Josh and the equally attachment-disordered Martha did in Scenario 2.

Your ex may be dastardly. He may behave in ways that would have driven even Mother Teresa into a murderous rage. Yes, you're entitled to your anger, your fear, your regret. But that's doesn't mean that acting on these feelings will be beneficial to you. You don't have to become Lady Macbeth or Martha.

Be honest with yourself: Are your reactions more than what is called for, given your circumstances? What roles do your anger and bitterness serve?

CHAPTER FOUR

The Role of Shame in Divorce

I f guilt could talk, it would say, "I did a bad thing." It's a healthy response, the first step toward accountability. It signals to us that we've done something that's hurt someone so we can make an amends, change our behavior, and move on.

If shame could talk, it would say, "I *am* bad." It's a toxic response, because it's tough to get rid of something that feels like an intrinsic part of who you are.

Divorce ignites shame, which is the reason why people with personality and attachment disorders have extreme reactions to it. And because the shame of a failed marriage feels intolerable to them, they often project it onto others, thinking or claiming, or both: "You're crazy (or evil, stupid, and a multitude of other undesirable traits)! The divorce is all your fault! Your terrible parenting is damaging our kids!" The one-sidedness of the thinking is a recipe for conflict.

Blame and anger serve a purpose for this HCP, who thinks, *If I continue to blame my circumstances on you, I can buffer myself against shame. I don't have to look at my part in problems. I don't have to change my behavior. I don't even have to grieve the loss of my marriage—after all, why would I miss someone who's a despicable person?*

CHAPTER FIVE

Grief and Divorce Your Life Wasn't Supposed to Be Like This

Divorce is like a death. With it your vision for your life disintegrates and you're thrust into the unknown. People need to grieve the end of their marriages the way they'd grieve the loss of someone they loved.

Swiss psychiatrist Elisabeth Kübler-Ross, M.D., developed a five-stage theory for how we move through grief. At intervals, people usually experience:

- **Denial.** "Divorce sucks, so I won't accept it."
- **Anger.** "Divorce sucks, it's your fault."

- **Bargaining,** "Divorce sucks, so I'm going to keep the marriage alive by obsessing about it and what you or I could have done to save it."
- **Depression.** "Divorce sucks, life sucks, why bother with anything?"
- **Acceptance.** "Divorce sucks, but now that I accept that it happened, I can move on."

Of course, grief isn't a linear process. You don't trot through each stage chronologically and at a tidy clip or get a diploma when you graduate. You may reach acceptance then find that bargaining rears its ugly head years later during an important life event when you catch yourself thinking, *If only the marriage had worked, I would be holding your hand during our daughter's wedding instead of sitting next to you and your new wife, who, by the way, seems to be using Botox as a face cream.*

Divorced people need to go through the grief process in order to accept reality, stop blaming everything on their exes, and create new, meaningful lives. Blame and anger keep people from completing the grief cycle. They use dysfunctional strategies to defend against shame and loss. People carry on a relationship with their exes by obsessing about them and their ninety-seven terrible qualities.

Even when a legal divorce is final, the emotional divorce often isn't. Two people who are no longer in a physical relationship can remain psychologically entangled—in a weird way, making them still effectively "married."

CHAPTER SIX

High-conflict Divorce Is Addictive

Pe.ople involved in high-conflict divorce behave like addicts. But instead of organizing their lives around drugs or alcohol, they organize their lives around their ex. They're in pursuit of things that are elusive: trying to control the ex or give him a personality transplant—or her an epiphany so she sees the error of her ways. The more their efforts fail, the more energy they expend in their futile endeavors.

Why do they do this? Why, dare I ask, might you? The American Society of Addiction Medicine offers an explanation:

Addiction is a primary, chronic disease of brain reward, motivation, memory, and related circuitry. This is reflected in an individual pathologically pursuing reward and/or relief by substance use or other behaviors.

Addiction is characterized by the inability to consistently abstain, impairment in behavioral control, craving, diminished recognition of significant problems with one's behaviors and interpersonal relationships, and a dysfunctional emotional response.[1]

Let's examine what this type of emotional addiction looks like in an actual person. My client Jane, a forty-year-old attractive, smart professional and mom of two young children, was preoccupied with psychoanalyzing her narcissistic ex. She couldn't control her compulsive attempts to turn him into an empathetic person and child-centered father.

Every session, she would read me their latest email exchanges. He would invariably write something harsh and condescending, and she would follow suit with a lengthy response pointing out the error of his parenting ways and also using the "I statements" she'd learned in their earlier couples therapy to tell the person who didn't care about her feelings exactly how he was hurting her feelings!

As you can imagine, her approach didn't go as she hoped. It invited ridicule, contempt, and a nasty refusal to consider her point of view and requests. But instead of looking at what she was doing to incite conflict, Jane became more obsessed with the way her ex's mind worked. And our conversations, every session, would go something like this:

Jane: "Why does he act this way?"

Me: "Because he's a narcissist."

Jane: "But I just want to understand why he does the things he does. I want to figure him out."

Me: "You've already figured him out, Jane. He's a narcissist. You could write a dissertation on what makes him tick, and that's not going to make him change. So why waste your energy analyzing him?"

Jane: "I think it would give me closure."

Me: "Maybe for five minutes. But your brain is hooked on your ex, so you'd start obsessing again. Your energy would be better served learning to unhook yourself."

If we look at Jane's behavior through an addiction lens, we can see that she was *pathologically seeking rewards and relief*. She was seeking closure, her ex's respect, his transformation into an empathetic human being. Despite the fact that she never got any of these things (and just pissed him off whenever she tried), *she couldn't stop acting on her cravings*. She didn't recognize that her preoccupation with her ex was actually a *dysfunctional emotional response* that had a *negative impact on her daily functioning*. It made her depressed and anxious. Most significantly, it sapped the energy required to reboot her career and generate income that would offset the inadequate child support her ex was sending her. Even when she was able to recognize that her pursuits were futile, she was *unable to abstain* from obsessing about her ex or from sending him emails that triggered more of the behavior that made her nuts.

Clinically, Jane was not a high-conflict personality. She had a mostly secure attachment style and she was not a manipulator. Although she was stuck in an addictive pattern of reacting to her ex, after a while she was able to emotionally disengage from him.

How did she do it? She concentrated on examining her own thoughts and behaviors and changing the ones that no longer served her. She got a new job, began dating, and moved on with her life.

CHAPTER SEVEN

Failure to Master the Developmental Task of Divorce

If you're stuck in a high-conflict divorce, you may be thinking that what happened to Jane could never happen to you. Perhaps your ex is way worse than hers, you're always being dragged into court, and your kids are coming unglued.

As overwhelming as your circumstances might feel, focusing on them will keep you from "moving on," that mystical outcome that people keep telling you to achieve. You may feel like hitting them over the head with a hammer. They don't get it! Sure, you want to move on, but how do you do that when you have a diabolical ex who keeps dropping bombs in your life?

You will do it, not by controlling your ex, but by completing the psychological process I mentioned in the Introduction, the developmental task of divorce.

Erik Erikson's Theory of Human Development

After years of studying and working with high-conflict situations, I've come up with a theory of divorce based on the work of twentieth-century developmental psychologist Erik Erikson. But in order to fully understand the developmental task of divorce, you first need to understand Erikson's theory of how human beings develop. (Fun fact: Erikson coined the phrase *identity crisis,* and divorce, as we will learn, is a crisis of identity).

Erikson believed that two opposing *values* occupy each stage of life and, as individuals, we must need to understand and accept both for the optimal *virtue* to emerge as the best choice. As with personality disorders and attachment theory, Erikson's work is vast (he also won a Pulitzer Prize for it). You can read more about it on the internet, but for now, here's the *Reader's Digest* version.

- **Trust vs. Mistrust (birth to eighteen months).** If the baby trusts that his primary caregivers will take care of him, he develops a sense of trust that becomes the foundation for identity. If his parents are unreliable, he will perceive the world as being an inherently unsafe place. *Success in this stage = hope.*

- **Autonomy vs. Shame (one to three years).** The child starts to be independent and his parents must help him master certain basic tasks, such as toilet training. If the parents cheer him on, the child feels good about his exploration and feels safe to make mistakes. If the parents pressure him or make him feel that he's failed, the child will experience shame and worry about completing future tasks. *Success in this stage = will.*

- **Initiative vs. Guilt (four to five).** If the child is encouraged to do age-appropriate things on his own (for example, get dressed, make the bed, play with peers), he will develop confidence in his ability to lead. If the child is not allowed to make these decisions independently (think "helicopter parents"), he will believe he's incompetent and become a follower. *Success in this stage = purpose.*

- **Industry vs. Inferiority (six to eleven).** The child begins to compare himself to his peers; how he sees himself in relation to others impacts his self-esteem and sense of agency. Parents and teachers who encourage the child increase his feelings of competency. Restrictive parents can lead a child to doubt his abilities. The child who learns to balance these two extremes develops a sense of competence. *Success in this stage = competence.*

- **Identity vs. Role Confusion (twelve to eighteen).** The adolescent struggles to construct his identity: *Who am I? What do I believe in? What do I want to do in life? Where do I fit in?* Parents who allow their adolescent to explore their sense of self facilitate the child's identify formation. Parents who pressure the child create identity confusion. Fidelity (aka loyalty to an idea or a person) is the optimal virtue of this stage and arises when a child develops the ability to commit to others and accept differences. *Success in this stage = fidelity.*

- **Intimacy vs. Isolation (eighteen to forty).** The focus of young adulthood is to form close relationships, both with friends and romantic partners. When people feel connected to others, they experience a sense of safety and belonging. Those who are unable to form lasting relationships generally feel isolated and alone in the world. *Success in this stage = love.*

- **Generativity vs. Stagnation (forty to sixty-five).** In the second stage of adulthood, people are either making progress in their careers or floundering. They may be married, raising children, and active members of their community . . . or not. If the adult knows what he cares about and is living in alignment with his values, he feels productive. If the adult regrets his decisions, he may lack a sense of purpose. *Success in this stage = care.*

- **Integrity vs. Despair (sixty-five-plus).** In this last stage of life (according to Erikson), people reflect on what they did and didn't achieve. Feeling guilt and remorse about the past leads people to feel despair. Integrity comes from accepting life in its entirety: both its victories and its losses. The wisdom that comes from completing this developmental task allows for a sense of serenity when considering the prospect of death. *Success in this stage = wisdom.*

People who have successfully completed their appropriate developmental tasks before they get a divorce generally have an easier time rebuilding their lives afterward. They are more likely to move on and even feel unencumbered and excited about having the opportunity to try new things and meet new people. They still feel like themselves—or at least like new versions of themselves.

The truth is that divorce prompts an identity crisis for everyone. Temporarily, as your social role shifts, you have to find new ways of defining yourself to yourself. But personal growth work is a good thing! You're free from the albatross of a bad marriage. You can do what you want when you want and with whomever you want. However, the crisis is deeper and longer lasting for those who didn't master the developmental tasks of early life stages.

The Psychosocial Developmental Task of Divorce

After several years of treating clients going through high-conflict divorce, I started to recognize a predictable pattern of behavior. These people were *stuck.* They couldn't seem to disentangle themselves from their exes, and often, from the routines of their former married lives. Even if they had remarried, re-procreated, and re-friended, they were *still* preoccupied with blaming their exes for their current problems and dissatisfaction. For the people who hadn't gone on to something better and were basically treading water, the preoccupation was even more extreme.

These clients reminded me of what I referred to in the Introduction as failure-to-launch young adults: twentysomethings who point fingers at their parents for the fact that they're not where they'd hoped to be. It occurred to me that failure-to-launch divorced people are a lot like failure-to-launch young adults. Why?

Because they hadn't mastered the developmental task of divorce.

While a divorce can happen during many stages of life, transcending it requires the same balancing act as in Erikson's theory of human development. Divorced people need to learn how to balance two opposing sets of *values* in order to develop the *virtue* that will enable them to continue moving forward successfully in life as an emotionally secure individual.

With many thanks to the great Erik Erikson for laying the groundwork, I'd like to present my theory of the developmental task of divorce.

Blame vs. Accountability. People going through divorce start out blaming the ex for the demise of the marriage and the difficulties in the present. If they're able to shift their focus to what they can do *now*, they can start taking accountability for their own choices, both past and present. Those who continue to marinate in blame give their power away. Those who admit their mistakes and acknowledge their ex's good points (everyone has some), while taking full responsibility for their own behavior, take back their power. *Success in the stage of divorce = empowerment.*

So, let's talk about *you* for a moment. Even if your ex is flat out crazy and breathtakingly evil, blaming him (or her) does you no good. Blame—especially if it is expressed via venting to friends, family, or the babysitter—may *temporarily* offload your frustration, but it won't fix your problems. In fact, it's likely to create more of them.

When you allow yourself to wallow in blame, you're not living well. You're obsessed with the past, which you can do nothing about. You're probably worried about the future too. For example: *If I don't agree to split the cost of yoga camp, she might drag me back to court to increase child support!*

Now you feel crappy most of the time. You have trouble sleeping. You gag when you try to eat, or you ingest a couple dozen more peanut butter cups than necessary. You're distracted at work (*All this stress is going to make me lose my job*) and, at home, you're snapping at your children. You don't enjoy hanging out with friends, going to the movies, or reading that new book by your favorite author because your divorce is taking up so much room in your head. So much room, in fact, that you can only calm down with help from your new BFFs, Xanax and Merlot.

See where I'm going with this? Getting over divorce is not about your ex. It's about changing your mindset. At the risk of sounding annoyingly new-agey, divorce really is an opportunity for personal growth. It's a crucible in which your character defects can be burned off, and new, positive traits can emerge.

If you blame your ex for your problems, you won't grow. But if you heed the invitation to grow and take responsibility for generating your own outcomes and fulfillment, you're more likely to achieve Divorce Nirvana: the ability to move on with your life.

Growth is much easier to do when we're not feeling threatened and pressured. In Part Two, we'll talk about skills that are useful for managing the crises of high-conflict divorce.

PART TWO

STRATEGIES FOR MANAGING YOUR HIGH-CONFLICT DIVORCE

CHAPTER EIGHT

Focus on Changing Behavior

When I was doing my clinical training for my marriage and family therapy licensure, I took a family therapy course taught by a wise and hilarious therapist who preached an active approach to the work. The other interns and I would present our cases to Rose and ask her expert advice on how we could help our clients gain insight. If they just got insight, we figured, they'd be able to change their lives.

One day as we nervous newbies were fretting about how to make the light bulb go on over our clients' heads, Rose uttered words I've never forgotten. *"People don't change because they get insight. They change their behavior and* then *they get insight."*

The room went silent. We all stared blankly at one another. Shifting our approach away from insight-oriented therapy was a radical notion. How could people change if they didn't understand why they did the things they did? What would motivate them?

"Stop thinking that way," Rose insisted. "Just get them to *do* something, even if the only thing you can get them to do is to swap places on the couch. Taking an action is the first step of change. After they change, even a tiny bit, you can talk about insights they've gained as a result."

After practicing therapy for a decade and a half, I can confidently confirm that Rose was absolutely right. You can plumb the depths of your tortured psyche for years and still not change. You probably know people like that—the therapy lifers. They go to counseling religiously, have financed the private school tuition of their therapist's kid, and they *still* act crazy.

Similarly, you can plumb the depths of your ex's tortured psyche for years and you're not going to make him or her change. Not only will you not make your ex-spouse change, but your post-divorce relationship also won't get any better.

The only way it will get better is if you do things differently.

The only person's behavior you can improve is yours.

Before we embark on strategies for managing a high-conflict divorce, I want to share another Rose story, for comic relief.

Crazies, Assholes, and Bitches

Before my mentor Rose moved to Los Angeles, she had a successful practice in an upscale New England neighborhood. Her specialty was divorce. Through her work with divorced families, she started noticing a pattern.

"They all said the same things about each other," she told me. "The ex-wife was crazy, the ex-husband was an asshole, and the new wife was a bitch. After a while, I started to realize, they can't *all* be crazy or assholes or bitches. It's just not statistically possible. There's something about divorce that makes people go nuts temporarily."

I agree—*and* I would make a distinction. I think most people go nuts during divorce, but it's not always temporary. Some people, frankly, were always nuts, even before the divorce. Some people, the difficult, unreliable, and manipulative ones we've talked about, the ones with personality disorders, the ones with attachment disorders, the ones who have struggled to master their developmental tasks, *these* people get exponentially nuttier after divorce. And they can stay that way for a very long time.

Maybe forever.

If you're reading this and you've identified that you have some issues, there is hope for you, but you will need to do some work on yourself. That means getting brutally honest about your own shortcomings—distorted thinking, emotional reactivity, and destructive behaviors—and changing them through behavior modification. Does that sound like a tall order? Part Three will guide you through this crucial process of personal growth.

And remember, if you've gone nuts and are feeling a little crazy or bitchy due to your divorce, there is a route to get back to sanity: being accountable for your own actions.

Let your ex do your ex.

You do you.

So, if this is your situation, if you're divorced from someone who's a little or a lot nuts, you need to change the way you interact with him or her. Perhaps the single most important thing you can do is to develop an effective communication strategy.

CHAPTER NINE

The BINF Communication Protocol

P oor communication drives high-conflict divorce. And by *poor communication,* I don't mean people making spelling errors and dangling their participles. I mean, people turning words into weapons that they unleash on one another to express their wounded feelings and do damage. If you're divorced from a HCP who's riling you up with nasty or manipulative remarks, don't despair! And don't fight fire with fire, as that will only make things worse. Instead, dampen the flames of your conflicts by adopting a special communication protocol that I have modified from one developed by the brilliant high-conflict strategist Bill Eddy.

Keep emails, texts, phone calls, and in-person interactions:

- **Brief:** Resist the urge to counter your ex's histrionic novella by cataloging all of his character defects and bad behavior in a 1,000-word email designed to set him straight once and for all. Write only what needs to be written. The less you say, the less your ex has to respond to. The same goes for unavoidable in-person interactions. When crossing paths at your child's soccer game, smile politely and move on.

- **Informative:** Think like a reporter, stating only the facts when you communicate. Facts do not include opinions, criticism, parenting advice, psychoanalysis, or an airing of trampled-upon feelings. Facts involve only the who, what, when, where, and how of a situation. For example: "Jonah's soccer game has been rescheduled to Sunday at 10 a.m. at Pan Pacific Park. He's carpooling with Ben's mom." Facts are much less likely to invite vitriol, or at least not as much as your opinions, which your ex doesn't care about.

- **Neutral:** I've changed Bill Eddy's original acronym from BIFF, with the first F indicating "friendly" to BINF, with an N for "neutral." I think writing and speaking in a friendly tone to someone who wants to rip you into teeny pieces is a stretch. A neutral tone is a lot more achievable and believable. Neutral expression includes no sarcasm, hostility, guilt tripping, or passive-aggression. It also means no emotion, so eliminate stylistic elements that deliver a punch and are sure to invite counter-punches. When writing a BINF-styled email, use no bold face, italics, colored fonts, all caps, or exclamation marks. In fact, try to extract all personality from your message. This is one time it's actually good to be boring.

- **Firm:** You should aim to minimize engagement. Do not engage in protracted negotiation. If your ex wants to swap visitation weekends on a weekend that doesn't work for you, politely decline, citing the court order (hopefully you have one). Don't waffle when your ex sends you seventeen emails trying to badger you into the swap. You've set a limit, so stick to it. If you were accommodating during your marriage, staying firm is likely to feel unnatural and scary at the beginning. However, it's imperative that you signal to your HCP ex that you have relinquished your role as a human doormat.

Now that you have the basics, here are some more high-conflict communication dos and don'ts I recommend.

Do:

- Wait until you're calm before writing or speaking with your ex.
- Ask a friend to read your ex's emails if reading them makes you gag.
- Write a draft, of an email wait twenty-four hours, then edit it using the BINF protocol.

Don't:

- Respond to emails or texts from your ex more than once a day.
- Write or phone your ex when you're angry.

Try to persuade your ex to think or do anything.

CHAPTER TEN

Understanding the Online Disinhibition Effect Or Why Your Ex Acts Like a Troll

High-conflict divorce isn't new, of course, but the dependence on electronic communication that has exploded in the last two decades has made it easier for exes to engage in psychological warfare.

John Suler, Ph.D., a psychology professor at Rider University, has spent his career studying the internet's impact on human behavior. His theory of the *online disinhibition effect* explains the ways the internet breaks down social conventions that are normally present during in-person interactions.

According to Suler, six factors create disinhibition.[1] These beliefs, usually subconscious, are:

- **Anonymity.** "You don't know me."
- **Invisibility.** "You can't see me."
- **Asynchronicity.** "See you later."
- **Solipsistic introjection.** "It's all in my head."
- **Dissociative imagination.** "It's just a game."
- **Minimization of status and authority.** "Your rules don't apply."

The disinhibition effect is most commonly used to describe the emotionally rabid behavior of online "trolls," people who leave inflammatory comments on internet articles or tweet death threats to public figures they don't like.

Hostile exes can act like trolls in online social networks. While Suler's anonymity factor isn't an issue here (obviously former spouses know each other), the other factors *are*, especially the "You can't see me," "See you later," and "Your rules don't apply" factors.

Angry divorced people can feed off the lack of real-time risk inherent in cyber communication. A normally passive individual might feel emboldened to write things they'd be too afraid to say to their ex in person. And a person who's aggressive by nature has an easy way to bully their former spouse. Most of us, in fact, have had an experience of letting impulse override reason when emailing someone who's made us mad or frustrated.

But when you're chronically mad and frustrated while playing the high-stakes game of divorce, emailing and texting just replaces the in-person fights you had during your marriage and divorce proceedings and it may even make them worse due to the online disinhibition effect.

Remember borderline Josh and narcissist Martha? Josh was devastated when Martha, pregnant with his child, ran off with her affair partner, Declan. As a borderline personality, Josh struggles with impulse control on a good day. Now, with his emotions heightened, facing the loss of his wife and unborn child, Josh unleashes his pain around the clock in 1,000-word single-spaced emails and rat-a-tat texts to the woman who torpedoed his world.

Here's an example.

You disgust me. You're a stupid, selfish whore. You're not fit to be a mother! That moron you shacked up with is a pothead. The two of you are probably just having sex and smoking weed all day. Do you think that's a decent environment for a child? But you're not thinking, are you? You're too busy screwing and getting high! Don't kid yourself, Martha, you'll never get away with this! The judge will see you for who you are, a slut and a miserable excuse for womankind. After I get full custody, you'll never see the baby again!

While Martha doesn't have Josh's impulse control issues, she can't tolerate feeling inferior, so she has to set Josh straight. Here's her email response.

Don't you dare speak to me that way! All you are is a sperm donor, so don't flatter yourself. No judge would allow a child to be raised by a mentally ill father. Thank god the baby will have a real man to look up to. You're clearly psychotic. Declan and I are model citizens, we would never be intoxicated around our child (and when I say 'our,' I mean Declan's and mine). We also wouldn't have sex around our child—but when we do make love, it's mindblowing! Declan knows how to please me in ways you never could. Anyway, the baby is going to have a fabulous life, one that doesn't include you! Buh-bye, loser!

Can you see the disinhibition effect playing out in these ex-spouses' email exchange? It's much easier for Josh and Martha to unload on each other because they're not face to face ("You can't see me"), they don't have to worry about an instant response ("See you later"), and the virtual nature of the exchange—which takes place by email or text— leaves them unfettered by pesky social norms and expectations ("Your rules don't apply").

The disinhibition effect distorts reality. People stop having dialogues. They don't listen or empathize. They don't see the impact of their behavior on the other. They become irrational, histrionic, and when greeted with a response they don't like, highly reactive.

Did you notice there are no *facts* in Josh and Martha's emails? There are plenty of opinions, posturing, insults, and threats, but no *information* that needs to be stated. Because this is the manner in which these two communicate, their hostility and conflict grows—and so do their legal fees. They can't resolve anything, so they fight over everything: community property, child custody, and child support. As long as Josh and Martha stay emotionally invested in punishing and rejecting the other, they'll never get "divorced," especially with a child they, theoretically, must raise together.

CHAPTER ELEVEN

Managing the Trauma of Your Divorce

D
ivorcing a high-conflict spouse can feel like living in a war zone. You never know when a bomb is going to go off, so you're constantly on high alert. It's important to know how your body reacts to chronic stress, so here's a mini-neurochemistry lesson.

Cortisol is a vital hormone produced and secreted by the adrenal glands, which are located on the tops of your kidneys. Cortisol levels peak in the morning, to get you out of bed, and decline as the day wears on, so you can fall asleep. Cortisol does good stuff, like helping you to maintain steady blood-sugar levels and fueling your brain. It's also an anti-inflammatory agent that prevents tissue and nerve damage.[1]

When you're under attack—either physically or psychologically—your cortisol levels surge. You need cortisol to give you the energy to cope with stress or flee from actual danger. Cortisol is great in the short term, but sustained release, in layman's terms, can really "f" you up. High-cortisol symptoms include:[2]

- Depression.
- Fatigue.
- Weight gain.
- Back pain.
- Trouble concentrating.
- Low libido.
- Acne.
- Impaired memory.
- Insomnia.
- Irritability.
- High blood pressure.
- Sugar cravings, of the kind leading you to ingest a box of Thin Mints or a whole large pepperoni pizza at one sitting.

Too much cortisol scrambles the body's stress response system, which helps us respond optimally to stressors. If you find yourself overreacting to relatively benign events—for instance, having a panic attack when you hear the ping of an email arriving on your phone—this is a sign of *cortisol dumping.*

Cortisol dumping is a major player in the traumatic stress associated with divorce. High cortisol levels hijack your brain and cause you to have kneejerk reactions to input instead of having reasonable responses. Classic divorce post-trauma symptoms include:[3]

- Ruminating about your ex's heinous behavior.
- Trouble sleeping and nightmares about your ex.
- Constant jitteriness.
- Mood swings.
- Hypervigilance (always waiting for the "other shoe" to drop).
- Engaging in hostile email and text communication.
- Raging.
- Difficulty with mundane tasks and basic decisions due to being overwhelmed by divorce.
- Feeling numb and disengaged.

Most people going through divorce experience trauma. Your life as you knew it is unraveling, after all. But when post-traumatic divorce stress goes on for more than six weeks, it can become a full-blown disorder, hence the moniker *divorce post-traumatic stress disorder* (PTSD).

In order to manage divorce PTSD—instead of it managing you—you need to develop *trauma resiliency skills*. You will have a hard time consistently applying the communication strategies and boundary-setting tactics outlined in this book if you don't first learn to calm down your overactive nervous system. It's kind of like being a dry drunk who, while abstaining from alcohol, still rages as if he were inebriated because he hasn't learned to be emotionally sober.

Trauma resiliency skills involve doing things to regulate your brain's stress response system, so you're in a state neither of *hyperarousal* (on high alert) nor of *hypoarousal* (numb and checked out). Here are some basic ways to manage divorce PTSD and restore your nervous system to baseline.

- **Set a divorce curfew.** *Do nothing related to your divorce after 8 p.m.* No emailing your ex or your attorney, no preparing legal documents, no rehashing the latest installment in your divorce saga over the phone to friends. Admittedly, there may be times when you have to do divorce stuff at night (say, if you're on a court-imposed deadline). But as a general rule, set your divorce aside so your cortisol levels will drop, and you can get a decent night's sleep.

- **Eat sanely.** The stress of high-conflict divorce can make it hard to eat. Some people shed weight they don't need to lose because they're too emotionally overwrought to think about meals. Others pack on the pounds by stuffing their feelings with the latest sugary treats from Trader Joe's. Either way, you're throwing your blood sugar levels off-kilter and making it hard for your brain to function. Eating regular, small, protein-rich meals will stabilize your blood sugar and energy. If you gag at the thought of food or find the prospect of preparing it overwhelming, have easy foods on hand, like hard-boiled eggs, nuts, and cheese sticks.

- **Practice good sleep hygiene.** Sleep deprivation will make everything seem worse. It's like taking the express train to depression and anxiety, especially if poor eating has already compromised your ability to function. Getting a good night's sleep is critical in managing symptoms of post-trauma, so cultivate good sleep hygiene habits: Go to sleep at the same time every night, try to make your bedroom as dark as possible, quiet any racing thoughts by listening to a meditation app or a white noise machine. Program your mind to associate your bed with sleep, so try to do work or watch TV in another room. The blue light emitted from computer and phone screens messes with your melatonin (sleep hormone), so don't look at those in the hour before bedtime. If your sleep hygiene protocol isn't enough to lull you to slumber, consider seeing a doctor for medication. For all those who hate the thought of taking psychotropic medication, you will not win any medals for toughing it out. Taking meds is better than enduring chronic insomnia.

- **Exercise.** Exercise is nature's mood stabilizer. So much so that psychiatrists usually tell patients with depression and mood disorders to exercise every day. If you can't manage daily workouts, then aim for three to four times a week. You don't have to do anything strenuous; twenty minutes of moderate exercise, such as walking, will do the trick. Another benefit of regular exercise is that it will help you sleep.

- **Resourcing.** If you've experienced divorce trauma, you may be on high alert most of the time. Things could be going swimmingly, but you're poised for disaster. To be blunt, you freak out over nothing or next to nothing. In order to assess reality accurately and function normally, you need to develop internal and external sources of safety. This is a fancy way of saying you need to identify ways to calm yourself down that do not include drugs, alcohol, sex with the wrong people, or bags of fun-sized candy. Here are two resourcing tools, one internal and one external.

  o *Grounding* is an example of an *internal resource* that's super easy to do. You simply look around, wherever you are, and focus on one object at a time. Then, either silently in your mind or aloud, you describe in detail what you see. For instance: "That wall clock is round, with a bright red rim, a white face, and black numerals in a modern-looking font." I think it's more effective to do this out loud, but if you're having an anxiety attack in a room full of people, you probably want to do it silently. Grounding is a simple, but powerful tool because it shifts your focus from worrying about the future or ruminating about the past to the present. It's a way of reassuring your mind that you're safe.

o *Seeking support* is an example of an *external resource*. You identify trustworthy people to talk to, or simply to be around, who will help you feel safe. You gain strength from comforting or inspiring people. They could be friends, relatives, a therapist, or a clergyperson. They should *not* be your children, your cousin Mabel who's still bitter about her divorce ten years ago, or anyone who's prone to catastrophizing. When you seek support from a trusted person, try not to talk endlessly about your evil ex. Retelling your problem story will just retraumatize you, and the goal of resourcing is to shift your focus *away* from the trauma so you can develop felt states of safety. Share just enough information so your support people understand what's going on. You may not need to say anything at all; being around someone who makes you feel good may be enough.

- **Trauma-informed therapy.** For more guidance and support developing trauma resiliency skills, see a therapist who specializes in trauma. A trauma specialist may offer more sophisticated tools, such as *eye movement desensitization and reprocessing* (EMDR), a protocol designed to alleviate the distress and hyperarousal caused by traumatic memories, and *somatic experiencing,* an intervention aimed at releasing physical tension that remains in the body after a traumatic event. Trauma specialists prioritize physiological desensitization—getting less stressed out— over talking. The idea is that you need to be able to calm down and stop reacting to bad memories so you can talk about them without retraumatizing yourself.
- **Breathwork.** Talk therapy doesn't work for everyone. And I say that as someone who is primarily a talk therapist! Some people need to experience things physically in order to think differently and change their behavior.

Breathwork is a breathing technique that helps people work through trauma. It does not depend on conscious thought, so it gets around the defense mechanisms that perpetuate poor choices. For example, the thought: *My ex is such an asshole that I'm justified telling him off in an email or wasting an entire afternoon pacing around the house and ruminating about the ways he's wronged me.* Breathwork is becoming a popular alternative treatment for addiction, trauma, and other mental health issues. You can find programs offered in Southern California, New York, and Arizona. (See Resources.)

Withdrawing from the High of High-conflict Divorce

PTSD changes the mind. Kevin Gilmartin, Ph.D., a behavioral scientist who studies the effect of chronic stress on law-enforcement professionals, likens the biochemical response in life-threatening situations—increased alertness, awareness, and the flight-or-fight reaction—to "taking a bunch of uppers."[4] No wonder, then, that police officers become addicted to dangerous situations. Leaving the office and returning home, Dr. Gilmartin writes, is like taking "a bunch of downers."[5]

You'd think that a respite from crisis would be a relief, but sometimes it's *too* much of a relief. As hypervigilance ebbs, cops experience "detachment, exhaustion, apathy, and isolation."[6]

This seesaw of intensity is almost identical to that of high-conflict divorce. Your nervous system goes into overdrive when you read your ex's latest email, threatening to modify custody, yet again. When you find out it's an empty threat this time, you're relieved, but exhausted. Many people with bad divorces become addicted to their rage. Anger feels better than the depression and emptiness they feel when they go home alone.

Let's take a look at Gilmartin's descriptions of the so-called *lethal triad* of police work, which is also present in bad divorces.[7]

- **Isolation.** Cops get burned out and withdraw from social engagements due to exhaustion. In the case of high-conflict divorce, people withdraw due to shame. Cutting off contact with others means that you are left to handle emotional challenges without support.

- **Anger.** Cops and people with high-conflict divorces get angry because life is not as it should be. Cops watch civilians do horrible things to each other. Divorced people watch their exes do horrible things to get back at them. Cops chafe under the often ineffective management of their supervisors. Divorced people fume at the highly subjective and unpredictable nature of family law, which often leads to rulings that burden the more vulnerable spouse or fail to adequately protect children.

- **Projection of blame.** Both cops and high-conflict divorced folks blame people and events they can't control for their problems. They do this to "the point where they feel totally overwhelmed and incapable of addressing their issues."[8]

Gilmartin teaches trauma resiliency skills to law enforcement professionals, but his theory applies just as much to survivors of a high-conflict divorce. He believes that emotional survivors—those that manage chronically stressful situations with most of their marbles intact—are multidimensional people. If you're a cop, this means being more than just a cop—having family and hobbies unrelated to policework. If you're a divorced person, this means having a life beyond your divorce—other relationships and activities.

After you've separated, after the divorce is final, and even when no court battles are looming, your brain may still be poised for disaster. In order to move forward in your new life, you will need to grow a new brain. You will need to learn how to regulate your central nervous system, so it doesn't constantly have you prepped for disaster. You need to be able to shift from crisis mode to personal growth mode.

The 2008 film *The Hurt Locker* beautifully illustrates the challenges of withdrawing from conflict. Jeremy Renner plays an army specialist sent to Iraq to dispose of explosive devices. He seems emotionally impervious to the most hair-raising, risk-taking situations.

But when his mission is over and he returns to his family, he can't seem to "do normal." He's befuddled by the mundane task of choosing cereal at the grocery store. He struggles to connect with his wife and young son. His brain can't recalibrate to civilian life, with all its downtime and gray areas. Primed for danger, he heads out on another tour of duty.

People with high-conflict divorces can learn lessons from cops and veterans. If you truly want to transcend the acrimony in your life, you must get your biochemistry back in balance through developing emotional resiliency skills. You must take control of the things that you can.

Shifting from blame to accountability is the key to mastering the developmental task of divorce. When you stop thinking of divorce as the root of your misery and start seeing it as a jumping-off point for your own personal growth work, *then* you can create a more meaningful life than you ever had before.

CHAPTER TWELVE

Boundaries
Sweep Your Own Side
of the Street

Boundaries keep people safe. They clarify the line between you and someone else. Boundaries can be physical, sexual, financial, and emotional. For instance, you may be uncomfortable with someone standing close to you because when someone does you feel that your personal space is being invaded. Or you may feel uncomfortable if a friend asks to borrow money because you don't believe in mixing finances and friendship. Your discomfort with certain things that people do is associated with where your internal boundaries lie—which is different for all of us.

You get to say where a boundary is and when someone else has crossed it. Knowing when it has happened is easy for people who are clear about their boundaries. The problem is, many people aren't. Especially those who run around trying to make everyone else happy or typically twist themselves into pretzels to avoid conflict. They don't believe they're allowed to say no, or even recognize when they should.

If you have trouble recognizing and establishing your boundaries—communicating them effectively so people know what they are and will respect them—you are setting yourself up to have your boundaries violated. This can leave you feeling unsafe. Conversely, if you have trouble accepting other people's limits, you may threaten their sense of safety. It is one thing if you don't know what they are—after all, you're not a mind reader—and it is another thing if a boundary has been expressed and you refuse to respect it.

Most divorced couples with children struggle to adjust to the shifting boundaries in the relationship. If you have been the primary caregiver and you are now sharing custody 50/50, you will not have access to everything that goes on in your ex's house. In fact, you won't know *most* of what goes on in your ex's house—nor should you. Parents who interrogate their children after they return from the co-parent's home are violating their kids' emotional boundaries. Children should not feel compelled to divulge what Dad cooks for dinner or how Mom is spending the child-support money.

Your inability to accept that you can't know or control what goes on in your co-parent's home will increase conflict, make your kids anxious, and keep you in a perpetual state of inner turmoil. So, you need to work on acceptance if this is one of your issues.

Setting and maintaining boundaries will help you redirect your focus from your ex to yourself. It's a crucial step in managing divorce PTSD. For now, here are some things you can do to establish healthy boundaries between you and your ex.

- **Set a divorce curfew.** Stop doing, or talking about, anything related to your divorce by 8 p.m. As was discussed in Chapter 11, setting a curfew can help you to lower your levels of stress hormones. To reiterate, this technique means no emailing your ex, no preparing legal documents, no unleashing your divorce angst on the phone with friends. You need to calm your nervous system down in order to get a good night's sleep. And you need to be able to get enough sleep to keep from short circuiting your nervous system. In the few hours before bedtime, do things that have nothing to do with your divorce. Read your kids a story, listen to a guided meditation, take a bath. Your divorce will still be there tomorrow, so give it a rest for the night. My client Layla experienced a marked drop in her stress levels from diligently obeying this rule—so much so that when friends ask her about her divorce after 8 p.m., she would tell them: "I can't talk about it right now, I have a curfew!"

- **Don't play detective**. Part of accepting divorce (aka reality) is that you don't get to know what goes on in your co-parent's home. Unless you have evidence, or reasonable grounds, for suspecting abuse (in which case, you need to notify your attorney ASAP), you don't have the right to run a reconnaissance mission to keep tabs on your ex. After all, what's the point? You can't force him to abide by your parenting philosophy or keep her from having her new romantic partner over for Sunday dinner. Pressing your kids for details puts them in an unholy triangle with you and your ex; and having more information will just give you more to fume about. Divorce means that you aren't privy to things that you would be if you and your ex were still married. Does this suck? Yes. But continuing to fight reality will suck a lot more. Everyone has to (or should) let go of the reins when their kids become adults anyway; you're just getting a head start.

- **Follow the court order**. For amicable co-parents, the court order is a guideline they can modify as they see fit. You and your ex may be able to do that someday, but not now. For now, you need to follow the court order to keep chaos at bay. Adhere to the visitation schedule, pay child support on time, and do everything your divorce agreement tells you to do. If your ex is perpetually wandering off the reservation, notify the appropriate enforcers: your attorney or your local Child Support Services office.

- **Keep your opinions of your ex to yourself**. Children hear everything you say about your former spouse, even if you think you're saying it on the down-low, at the opposite end of the house, whispering behind the bathroom door. While it's appropriate to address a falsehood (more on that later), it's never okay to tell your kids you think their other parent is a "heinous excuse for a human being," or words to that effect. Even if they don't share your sentiments with your ex, they'll soak up your animosity and wonder if you feel the same way about them, since they share your ex's DNA. There's also the chance that they'll relay your feelings to your co-parent—especially if that co-parent is in the habit of grilling them when they return from your house.

- **Use the phone judiciously**. Many co-parents have a phone policy clause in their custody agreement specifying when they can call their children during the other parent's visitation time. Ostensibly, this policy is in the children's best interests, so kids have consistent contact with the parent they're not visiting. Too often, however, the phone policy serves to quell a parent's separation anxiety, interrupt the child's time with the co-parent, or foster a toxic triangle. For example: *"If you don't like what's going on at Dad's house, tell me, and I'll fix it!"* One call a day is plenty (and really, less is even better for older kids). Keep the conversation brief and the focus on maintaining contact—not on gathering intel on your ex.

If you're already enforcing these boundaries, but your ex just keeps steamrolling over them or delights in finding passive-aggressive ways to subvert your limits, you may be wondering how you'll ever be able to co-parent.

The truth is, you may *never* be able to co-parent.

Co-parenting requires two people who have the skills to resolve conflict and agree to alternative options. It also requires two people who can accept that while their ex's parenting style may be different, it will not actually screw up the kids for life or ruin their chances of getting into Harvard.

Attempts to co-parent with someone who is fundamentally incapable of co-parenting will inflame conflict. Co-parenting involves conversations, and conversations with a high-conflict personality aren't really conversations;

they're opportunities for debate, arguments, and drama.

So, if your question is: What do I do if co-parenting doesn't work? The answer is: You don't.

You learn how to parallel parent instead.

CHAPTER THIRTEEN

The Art of Parallel Parenting Different Rules in Different Houses

In early stages of child development, kids engage in parallel play. Picture two preschool children playing side by side in the sandbox. Owen is so engrossed in digging tunnels that he's unaware of Clarissa, who's loading up the sand pail next to him. Owen and Clarissa may spend their entire recess in the same sandbox and never interact with each other.

Parallel parenting is the grown-up, divorced version of parallel play. Instead of playing parallel sand games, Owen and Clarissa are now raising their kids as independently of each other as possible. They don't ignore their court order or each other's legal rights. They minimize contact and give up the fantasy that they can collaborate on anything.

Here are some suggestions for parallel parenting.

- Host separate birthday parties
- Attend separate parent-teacher conferences (if school policy allows)
- Use curbside or school dropoffs so you and your spouse don't have to see each other during visitation swaps
- Stop trying to sync parenting styles and practices
- Communicate only through a court-ordered messaging system, such as the Our Family Wizard® app. Due to the disinhibition effect, do your best to avoid regular phone calls, text messages, and emails. If you still have confusion about the danger of disinhibition, please reread Chapter 10.
- Don't try to troubleshoot your child's grievances in your co-parent's house *unless* there is physical evidence of abuse and/or a legitimate safety risk to your children—in which case, you should call your attorney ASAP.

A word of caution. Never tell a custody evaluator, court-appointed mediator, or parenting plan coordinator that you *can't* co-parent. You can discuss your co-parenting challenges, but by no means should you divulge that you're a parallel-parenting enthusiast. If you do, you will be labeled the "difficult one."

Unfortunately, the family court system doesn't recognize that parallel parenting is the only viable option for divorced couples that can't calmly and rationally co-parent. Thus, judges mandate procedures such as mediation and family counseling for high-conflict exes that are at best a waste of time, and often, an invitation to more conflict. If you're ordered to participate in one of these doomed endeavors, be cooperative, reframe the experience in your mind as an opportunity to cultivate patience, and keep your opinions about parallel parenting to yourself.

The key to parallel parenting is to develop the proper mindset. You must accept the reality that you and your ex are not cut out to co-parent together. You don't have to like this fact; but refusing to accept it will just keep you spinning on the hamster wheel of high-conflict communication. Once you stop trying to push your square peg of a divorce into a round hole, you will feel more comfortable employing techniques that are outside the scope of conventional divorce wisdom.

CHAPTER FOURTEEN

What to Do When Your Ex Badmouths You to Your Kids?

Another piece of conventional divorce wisdom that deserves to be jettisoned is the ignore-what-your-ex-says-about-you mantra. The theory behind this commonly proffered advice is that defending yourself will confuse your children, who will eventually figure out the truth anyway.

Think about this for a moment. If you had a co-worker who was spouting egregious lies about you all over the workplace, would you keep your mouth closed while your reputation was being ruined? Would you just wait for your boss to "figure out the truth"? Probably not. You'd probably take your employer aside and explain your side of the story.

The same idea applies if your ex is badmouthing you to your children. High-conflict personalities want to undermine their kids' relationship with the other parent. One way to do this is to feed the children propaganda. You, the ex, are some combination of crazy, evil, and stupid. You're the one who wanted the divorce, messed up the marriage, and doesn't want the children to be successful for unknown, nefarious reasons.

Trying to thwart a child's relationship with a parent is a form of child abuse. Children have a right to love and be loved by both parents. Remember attachment theory? Kids need to form secure attachments to their parents in order to cultivate self-esteem and healthy relationships when they're adults. If your ex uses badmouthing as a weapon to weaken your bond with your child, he (or she) is guilty of emotional abuse. This is *not* the time to rise above it and cross your fingers that your kid will "figure it out." This is the time to intervene.

But intervene strategically.

Let's revisit Josh and Stella (his securely attached wife) for a moment. Borderline Josh defends against his abandonment issues and divorce shame by telling their five-year-old son Liam that Stella was the one who wanted the divorce and didn't try to make things work. Liam, understandably angry, relays this message to his mother.

Stella is furious, not just because badmouthing hurts Liam. She's also furious because she and Josh have a non-disparagement clause in their parenting plan, which orders both parties to refrain from speaking badly about each other to the children.

But instead of obsessing about things she can't control—like stopping Josh from slandering her or preventing Liam from siding with his father—she sets her frustration aside in order to have an appropriate conversation with her son.

Here is Stella's strategy.

- **She acknowledges Liam's feelings without getting defensive**. "You're really upset. This must have been hard for you to hear, and I understand why you're angry."

- **She presents her side of the story without debate or blame**. "I'm not sure why Daddy said that. But I can tell you what's true for me. I very much wanted our marriage to work. I felt that Daddy and I both tried in our own ways. There are some problems that even grownups can't fix. We couldn't figure out how to live together, so we got a divorce."

- **She teaches Liam relationship skills.** Parents "triangulate" their kids by using them as messengers to communicate to the other parent. When they do this, they model toxic relationship patterns. Triangles keep people from communicating directly; they erode boundaries and genuine intimacy. Stella teaches Liam healthy relationship skills by getting him out of the triangle: "If you have a question about me or you are upset with me for any reason, talk to *me* about it. Don't go to Daddy because the problem isn't between you and him. It's between you and me, and it's our job to fix it."

- **She teaches Liam critical thinking skills.** High-conflict personalities are black-and-white thinkers. They spew propaganda like politicians carrying out a smear campaign against their opponents. Instead of trying to prove why Josh is wrong, Stella helps Liam develop critical thinking skills so he can learn to form his own opinions. "Do you remember when you got upset with Sam because you thought he stole your Matchbox car? And then you found it later that day in your jacket pocket? You believed something that wasn't true because you didn't have all the information you needed to understand the situation. So that's kind of like this situation with what Daddy told you. You thought something was true that really wasn't because you hadn't heard my point of view."

- **She creates a sense of safety.** Stella knows that Liam doesn't feel safe to challenge his father. Josh's rigid worldview doesn't allow for dialogue. It's too scary to ask questions, so Liam agrees with Josh to avoid making him angry. Stella wants to create the opposite experience for Liam. She wants him to feel safe approaching her, so she encourages open communication: "You can talk to me about anything and ask me any questions. I may not have the answer, or I may not have the answer you want, but I will never get mad at you for wanting to talk, and I will never get mad at you for having your feelings."

- **Stella's body language matches her words.** *How* you say something matters just as much as *what* you say. If Stella were visibly angry or tearful when she talked to Liam, she would have confused him. He would have come away from the conversation wondering if she were telling the truth. He would have felt anxious. He certainly wouldn't have felt encouraged to approach her about anything he thought might upset her. Stella's ability to manage her own feelings, and keep an emotional charge out of her voice, makes it easier for Liam to listen to her. It also teaches him that people can talk about hard things without the world blowing up.

Stella's approach to dealing with badmouthing is effective because she focuses on what she can control. She recognizes that Josh, like many high-conflict personalities, will ignore the court order when it suits him because he believes his needs trump pesky rules. She realizes that the judge isn't going to follow Josh around 24/7 to enforce the non-disparagement clause, so dragging him into court is probably not going to make anything better (in fact, it will probably make things worse).

She doesn't counterattack by saying, *"Your father's a borderline nutcase and he should take his rightful place beneath the wheels of a bus!"* —although she may want to. She doesn't sink into passivity and sidestep the issue altogether. She understands that she's running a marathon, not a sprint. Working herself into a frenzy every time Liam parrots back Josh's propaganda will just sap her of her energy.

Instead of focusing on fighting Josh, Stella focuses on her parenting: validating her son's feelings; teaching him relationship and critical thinking skills; and modeling conflict resolution and healthy communication for him. Liam may not believe her when he's five. But as he shifts from being a concrete thinker to an abstract thinker, as most children do during adolescence, especially with added help from his mom, he may realize that his dad's "truth" is actually propaganda.

Well, that's great for Stella, you may be thinking. But what you do when your ex keeps violating court orders, dragging you back to court, or stirring up so much drama that legal action seems unavoidable?

CHAPTER FIFTEEN

Should You Litigate?

T he only thing you're certain to get in family court is answers—not necessarily justice. Whether you're initiating or responding to legal action, you must relinquish the fantasy that your judge is some omniscient and beneficent grandpa who will see through your ex's machinations and sanction him (or her) six ways from Sunday and grant you everything you deserve.

Despite what your well-meaning, but naïve friends and family might tell you, judges don't always rule on the side of common sense. In my practice, I've seen judges order struggling single parents to pay their gainfully unemployed exes child support. I've seen judges fail to grant restraining orders to spouses of violent offenders. I've seen judges award joint custody to egregiously neglectful parents and active addicts without reading declarations or custody evaluations that would prove to any reasonable person that these parents are truly unfit.

How does this happen?

Some judges are appointed to the bench without a solid grasp on family law. Some either don't take (or don't have) the time to read reams of documentation so that they properly understand the case. Many have biases that override reason.

I've also had clients bemoan the mid-case departure of a competent judge, who is then replaced by an irrational one.

Another reason the scales of justice may not be tipped in your favor: unethical or just downright lazy custody evaluators who don't interview collateral contacts—people who can vouch for your good character or attest to your spouse's lousy character.

Litigation tends to drag on. Cases get continued. It takes seventy zillion years to agree on a custody evaluator. The courts are backlogged due to budget cuts.

The process is brutal on your psyche, your finances, and especially, your children. You have to read heinous things your ex says about you, and write heinous things about your ex. You have to function at home and at work while the drama rages on. You hoped you'd gain control, but instead it seems like you're losing it.

Although you may feel sick and exhausted, a high-conflict ex could be energized by the fighting.

HCPs love attention and sashay into the courtroom like Vegas showgirls. Their moment has come; now they can tell *everyone* how crazy and unfit you are! Let the games begin!

The biggest problem with litigation is that it keeps couples psychologically *engaged* just as they're trying to dismantle their lives and disengage emotionally.

There are times when you simply *have* to litigate: If your ex poses a safety risk to your children, you can't resolve key issues out of court, or you need to relocate and want a move-away order.

Go to court if you must but be realistic about the outcome. For in-depth strategies on navigating the legal system when divorcing a high-conflict spouse, I highly recommend reading Billy Eddy's book *Splitting* (see Resources). It tells you exactly what proactive measures to take when family court is unavoidable.

Living with the constant threat of litigation, or actual court appearances, is traumatic. If you don't have a choice in the matter, you need to learn to manage your trauma so that it doesn't hijack your life. In fact, every person living with a high-conflict divorce would benefit from developing trauma resiliency skills.

PART THREE

TOOLS FOR YOUR EMPOWERMENT

CHAPTER SIXTEEN

Focus on What You Can Control

People who are undergoing or have undergone awful divorces, especially divorced people with children, have a tortured relationship with reality. And for good reason. It's no Sunday in the park having someone that you perceive to be a terrorist for a co-parent. One way of escaping the seemingly intolerable present is to indulge in fantasy.

In this type of fantasy, justice prevails. The judge sees your ex for the ridiculous human he is, grants you everything you're asking for, and orders your ex to pay your legal fees. Your children are immune to your former spouse's propaganda against you and recognize you for the loving parent you are—the parent they like best.

You construct the perfectly worded email that finally gives your ex an epiphany so that she changes her entire personality and realizes you're right about everything. Then your ex apologizes for all the ways she's wronged you and admits you're a superior human being.

The universe rewards you for the pain you've endured, bestowing upon you a victorious Wheaties box of a post-divorce existence: a happy second marriage, financial abundance, and well-adjusted children.

Karma catches up with your ex. His trophy wife leaves him. The kids turn against him. He flees the country, never to be heard from again.

The truth is, justice doesn't always prevail. And when it does, it can take a long time. Therefore, hitching your happiness to the whims of circumstance is simply not a good life strategy. Resenting your past and demanding a better future will do nothing but make you miserable, cranky, and insane.

Life isn't fair. It just isn't. You may not have been responsible for some of what's happened to you, but you *are* responsible for how you choose to deal with it.

"But, *but!*" I hear you protest. "How can I be happy when my ex keeps trying to punish me? I'm Mother Teresa and my ex is Hitler! Are you actually suggesting that the problem is *my* perspective?"

I am suggesting your perspective is a problem that has a solution.

I am proposing the revolutionary idea that your ex is not the source of your problems. *Your relationship to the present is.* Your thought patterns, defense mechanisms, and unhelpful behaviors were probably in existence well before your divorce, or even your marriage.

Even if your situation stays the same, your life will drastically improve *if* you change the habits that have nothing to do with your ex: the unskillful, unproductive ways you think and act. Your ex may have exacerbated these issues, but your spouse did not cause them.

This is actually good news. Because you can control your own choices. You cannot, *ever*, control your ex.

Repeat after Me: "I cannot, ever, control my ex"

Let these words be your mantra. Accepting the fact that you can't control your ex is the key that will free you from the claustrophobic emotional prison in which you've been living. Surrendering to reality may *feel* like defeat, but it's really a process of recalibrating your brain so you can live life on life's terms.

This doesn't mean you're passive. Quite the opposite. It means that you are relinquishing the pipe dream that your ex will ever be anyone other than who he or she is and actively focusing on things in your life that you can change.

CHAPTER SEVENTEEN

Radical Acceptance
Sometimes Life Sucks

In Buddhist philosophy, the process of surrendering to your present circumstances is known as *radical acceptance.* My clients who practice radical acceptance have evolved not in spite of their crappy divorces, but *because* of them.

High-conflict divorce is an ongoing crisis. It hurts you financially, emotionally, and physically. Relationships with your children may be damaged. Your ex's chaotic shenanigans may punctuate your daily life, making it hard for you to function and concentrate on anything other than your lousy divorce. People may pull away, overwhelmed by the intensity of being around you.

You probably feel anxious and depressed. You may feel so depressed, in fact, that you flirt with the idea of suicide. Not because you actually want to be dead, but because you can't fathom the thought of enduring more years that feel like today.

I'm not going to tell you that divorce or being a single parent doesn't suck, because it does. I'm not going to tell you that if you just "think positive" everything will turn out fine.

What I can tell you is that there *is* a way for you to be fine even with your crappy circumstances.

Amid the chaos surrounding you is opportunity. Opportunity to evolve. Opportunity to become a better person, parent, and professional. Opportunity to live better and love better.

In Part One, I introduced the concept of divorce as a developmental task. I explained that shifting from blame to accountability is essential in order for you to empower yourself. In Part Two, we explored strategic strategies that can help you navigate communication and co-parenting with your ex and handle being under pressure. In the remaining chapters of this book, I'm going to talk about tools and techniques for developing the skills of this phase of your life.

Remember that the developmental task of divorce is to shift from blame to accountability. Blame is seductive. It's a black-and-white concept that your anxious mind can wrap itself around. The certainty of blame distracts you from the uncertainty of your post-divorce life. It buffers you from the shame of an unsuccessful marriage, the pain of being single in a coupled-up world, and the agony of being unable to raise your kids exactly the way you'd hoped.

If you continue to succumb to the siren call of blame, you will never truly grow up. You will become a failure-to-launch divorced person. You will stay emotionally tied to your ex, the same way a failure-to-launch young adult insists that his parents are the reason he hasn't made more out of his life after his schooling has ended.

When you blame your unhappiness on your ex-spouse, you make your ex your higher power—a supernatural figure with a godlike ability to control you. You worship at the altar of resentment. You organize your thoughts around him or her—focusing relentlessly on the horrible things he or she has done and the horrible things he or she is bound to do.

But your ex is not your higher power. He or she is not the parent, and you're not the child. No matter what heinous hash your former spouse has slung at you, you're an adult and you must take full responsibility for your choices. When you do this, when you shift from blame to accountability, you empower yourself.

You master the developmental task of divorce.

Personal growth is a balancing act. In order to make things better, you must accept the way things are right now. Remaining entrenched in blame, by contrast, keeps you in a fight with reality. A fight you'll always lose. You cannot change reality: for example, the fact that you married the person you did or the fact that you can't control what your ex thinks or does.

Radical acceptance is the first step in mentally and emotionally transcending high-conflict divorce.

CHAPTER EIGHTEEN

Why You Need a Spiritual Practice, Even If You're an Atheist

Years ago, I asked a family law attorney known for being ruthless for the single most significant piece of advice she gives her clients. I was expecting to hear "Document, document, document" or "Don't cry in my office." Instead, she surprised me with this: *"I tell them to maintain their spiritual practice."*

This attorney had been through a bad divorce herself. Her ex-husband had gambled away their life savings and left her flat broke with three kids to raise. Somehow, she managed to put herself through law school and become a prominent family law attorney. She knew firsthand how destabilizing a divorce can be, especially when it strips you of financial stability, your identity, and your place in the world.

Medicating yourself with booze, shopping, Instagram feeds, and casual sex with sketchy people is certainly an option, but the prognosis isn't good for people who do such things to numb their feelings. Avoiding pain doesn't work for long. On this trajectory, you become increasingly more reliant on externals to change the way you feel. Running away from your feelings and circumstances causes more, and bigger, problems, such as addiction, subsequent failed relationships, and difficulty being present for your kids.

You will never feel grounded if you depend on externals for inner peace and happiness. The only way to feel sane is to connect to something the material world doesn't offer.

If the word *spiritual* is giving you the heebie-jeebies, I understand. I was a PK (preacher's kid) and my mother's parents were Christian missionaries. I spent every Sunday for the first thirteen years of my life squirming in a church pew and struggling to resonate with anything that remotely related to God. At fifteen, I went *mano a mano* with my parents and refused to set foot in church again or have anything to do with religion. It simply wasn't working for me.

I still don't believe in God, but I do believe in something greater than myself: a universal force that connects me to others and to a higher purpose beyond my desires and urges. And I promise you that the only things you need to have to transcend your divorce drama are a desire to return to sanity and a commitment to developing the skills required to do that.

People going through high-conflict divorces tend to organize themselves around their divorces. That means they obsess about their exes, spend a lot of time thinking about how they might control their exes, and react in ways that make things worse.

As I have said before, giving your ex that much attention means that you've made him or her your metaphorical higher power. In essence, your mind becomes conditioned to trying to understand the thoughts and behaviors of someone you loathe. As much as you hate giving your ex free rent in your head, you may continue to do it because it's familiar. It's easier to focus on the devil you know than the devil you don't know.

What it would really benefit you to figure out, as a newly single person, is stuff like who you are, the things you need to fix about yourself, and your future.

In order to release your obsession with your ex, you will need to swap it out for something more meaningful to your new situation. Otherwise it could make you anxious and it will leave a void that you'll be tempted to fill with various addictive behaviors.

Your spiritual practice is intended to replace your ex as a figure of prominence in your imagination. For our purposes, this practice will be a mindfulness practice.

Through a mindfulness practice, you surrender to the universal truth that suffering is an unavoidable part of life. Instead of running from, or resisting, inevitable pain, you sit with it. As you learn to tolerate feelings that once seemed intolerable, you'll realize that your relationship to people and events is the real culprit, not the people and events themselves. Your spiritual practice will help you change your relationship to the present so you can manage your emotions and make more mindful choices.

Here's a simple mindfulness practice I developed. It takes all of ten minutes, although spending more time on it is great. It's best if you do it in the morning, although it doesn't really matter *when* you do it as long as you practice at some point every day.

Your Daily Mindfulness Practice

This practice has four steps.

1. **Read something inspirational.** Pick a book to read that inspires hope and provides guidance on how to live wisely. Personally, I'm a huge fan of Anne Lamott, whose 2018 book,

Almost Everything, which contains her reflections on hope, is a great choice. For a nuanced lesson on mindfulness, Phillip Moffit's *Emotional Chaos to Clarity* is also good, though it's a tougher read. And I can't say enough good things about twelve-step literature. You don't have to be an addict to get something out of these books, which at essence are manuals on how to be a grownup. Anyway, once you've found a book, read a page or two to get in the right headspace for the rest of the practice.

2. **Write down five things for which you're grateful.** After you've done your reading, write a gratitude list. (Get a journal, because you're going to be writing a similar list every day from now on). Shoot for five items, although by all means don't stop there if you're feeling particularly appreciative on a given day. If you're miserable and can't think of anything good, jot down small things, like a hot shower, a firm mattress, having all your toes (assuming you have them). You will see that those "small things" are not actually so small, and that you've been taking a lot for granted. When you shift your thoughts from what you don't have to what you do have, your mood will improve.

3. **Write down five intentions.** Intentions are a bit different from goals. Goals are outcome

oriented, as in: "I want to lose ten pounds by tomorrow." Intentions are more about the journey and less about the destination. Write down five things you want to manifest in your life. And remember, these can be the same day after day or you can change them. Some examples: "I want to release fear and anger toward my ex," "I want to attract a healthy romantic partner," "I want to be present and enjoy my kid's childhood." You might also include things that benefit others, such as sending healing energy to a sick loved one or cultivating compassion for someone you find irksome—even, perhaps, your ex! Don't get bogged down today wondering how you're going to do these things, just write what you want to release or create in your journal.

4. **Reflect for at least three minutes.** This fourth step builds on the three that came before. When you did your inspirational reading and wrote your gratitude list, you prepared your mind for contemplation. When you recorded your intentions, you picked your focus for meditation. So now that you're in the right frame of mind and you're clear about what's important to you, close your eyes for three minutes and reflect on your intentions. If you can tolerate more time, great! And even if you're not in the right frame of mind for reflection yet, it's okay

because you tried, which is the most important thing. Do your best to visualize what you want happening. Fantasize about it, drawing upon all your senses. If you catch yourself craving a particular outcome, observe the physical and emotional energy that accompanies unrequited longing and turn your attention back to your intentions. The important thing is to focus on what you can control—the act of naming what you want—instead of obsessing about what you can't control, such as if and when the thing you want to happen actually happens.

Note: If you have a preexisting meditation practice, please do this visualization in addition to that practice.

What to Expect from Your Spiritual Practice

If you don't notice a change in your thoughts, feelings, and behavior after diligently following this four-step mindfulness practice for three days, three weeks, or three months, don't despair. And don't give up. Developing a spiritual practice (and changing years of mindless behavior) takes time. Just because you don't notice any big changes in your mood or silence of your obsessive thinking doesn't mean the practice isn't working. Keep at it. The "magic" isn't really that magical. It's the culmination of routine, repeating the same simple acts until they become a ritual.

My clients who have adopted this four-step daily practice tell me it's the most effective means they've found of transcending their divorce drama. Understanding high-conflict divorce and learning strategies to manage it is valuable but cultivating mindfulness skills will change your life. One day you'll realize you're not getting buffeted about by your ex's latest round of chaos the way you used to. That it takes less effort to stay grounded. Or that you respond to a hostile email with a straightforward reply.

The best part? Now that you're not hemorrhaging energy ruminating about your ex, you're able to take that energy and use it for things that matter: your career, a new relationship, your children, and that book you've meaning to write.

If you really get into the practice, then you might want to crank it up a notch. Recovering drug and sex addict Russell Brand says that he meditates in front of an altar lined with four lighted candles (one each for his connections to the Divine, family, work, and other people) and items that hold significance. For you, these items could be photos, mementoes, or anything you consider a good luck charm.

You don't need to go to a church or temple to engage in a spiritual practice, but you might find that certain places (including houses of worship, like these) help you connect to something greater than yourself. I discovered this for the first time when I was seventeen and stood on the actual footbridge that the Impressionist painter Claude Monet featured in his famous Water Lily series.

I was a moody, self-absorbed teenager prone to panic attacks. In spite of my less than sparkling personality, my parents sent me to France and Belgium for my high school senior project, which involved studying Impressionist art and writing a paper about it. Monet's country home in Giverny, France, now a museum, was being painstakingly restored and was not yet open to the public. Yet my sister (who lived in Europe at the time) managed to sweet talk an invitation for the pair of us to enter what appeared to be Paradise: a rambling, green-shuttered pink house surrounded by gardens bursting with irises tulips, and peonies.

Monet also built a water garden, where he painted images from his lily pond. I was there in April and wisteria had draped itself over the Japanese footbridge. My sister and I were the only ones in the garden, which felt like a secret world we'd slipped into. I walked to the top of the footbridge and gazed through the mist and the weeping willows, to the white and pink water lilies bobbing along the surface of the pond.

And as I stood there, imagining myself where Monet had sat in front of an easel a century before, no doubt having his own spiritual experience, I had one of my own.

I stopped brooding. My angst dissipated, as if carried away by the ripples below me. It was the first time in my seventeen tortured years that I felt in sync with the rhythm of life. My problems seemed blissfully insignificant as my teenage spirit connected to the vast, but gentle universal force that speaks to anyone who will listen.

I'd like to say that I cultivated a spiritual practice from that day forward, but I lapsed back into the fitful unease that was my most faithful companion. It took decades and an apocalyptic divorce to make me relinquish my cerebral cynicism, stop pretending that reality was anything other than it was, and connect on a daily basis with something greater than myself and my first-world problems.

That footbridge had a huge impact on my life. The research paper I wrote about it won me an English prize in high school for creative nonfiction. Although I'd always loved to write, the experience of penning that paper motivated me to pursue writing as a career (practicing therapy would come later) and eventually to produce this book that you're now reading. My point: *A spiritual experience always shows up in the material world.*

Maybe you've had your own footbridge experience. Whether you have a place you can go to in real time or a place you can conjure up in your head, situating yourself in a peaceful atmosphere can help you engage spiritually and transcend your divorce woes.

CHAPTER NINETEEN

Doing a Divorce Inventory

The purpose of doing a written divorce inventory is to identify your resentments, character defects, and fears so you can begin to release them. I've borrowed the idea from twelve-step programs in which the fourth step is to do a "searching and fearless moral inventory." If you're in a twelve-step program of any kind and have already worked a fourth step, doing one specifically on your divorce will come naturally.

A quick word about the concept of *character defects*. These are thought patterns and behaviors that don't serve you, or anyone else, well. Being divorced doesn't mean you're broken. Regardless of our relationship status, we all have things we could change about ourselves. One upside to divorce is that you have an invitation to change that you might not have if you'd stayed married.

Recovering addicts work the fourth step to stop blaming their problems on others and take accountability for their choices. Since high-conflict divorce is like an addiction, completing an inventory will help you break free from the compulsion to obsess about your ex, and the fall-out of your divorce.

Your thoughts determine your feelings. To change the way you feel, you need to change the way you think. The divorce inventory is a form of cognitive restructuring, which is a fancy way of saying making a change in mindset. Writing it on paper makes the information concrete and memorable—much harder to deny or dispute.

This activity will lead you from feeling like a victim to being accountable for your own life. When you're done, you'll be less identified with your problem story— "My ex ruined my life" —and more open to creating a new narrative that better serves you.

So, let's begin.

Grab a notebook and a cup of coffee or tea. Silence your cell phone and put it out of view. Then write down the name of anyone associated with your divorce whom you resent. Obviously, your ex will be number one. But who else makes your blood boil? Your attorney? Your former best friend? Your sister, who's always questioning your choices? Your children, especially if they have ever taken your ex's side?

After you've compiled your list, take one person at a time and then complete the answers to the prompts below, as follows.

- The focus of my resentment is . . .
- Because . . .
- My part . . .
- Fears my resentment stirs up are . . .
- What could I have done differently in the past or do differently now?

Remember, you're going to inventory each focus of your resentment, one at a time.

Let me be clear. This task is not an invitation to further demonize your ex, your lawyer, your former friends, and so forth. It's designed to help you see the part you are playing in your problems. You must be rigorously honest about *your own behavior* for the exercise to be effective. Hating and blaming your ex, being bitter about your divorce— these unproductive emotions and thoughts aren't doing anything to improve your life.

Here's an example of how to do an inventory.

1. Focus of resentment: Mike (ex-husband).

2. Because: He cheated on me. Maxed out a credit card in my name and left me with debt. Pays child support late. Sends me nasty emails. Badmouths me to the kids. Doesn't abide by the visitation schedule in our custody agreement.

3. My part: I didn't do anything to get cheated on, but I ignored my intuition for years. I colluded with

Mike's spending, instead of canceling my credit card (or asking the bank to change the account number), because I was afraid to make waves. I'm not responsible for his failure to pay child support on time. I get defensive and self-righteous when I respond to his emails. Sometimes I badmouth him too. I'm not responsible for his belief that he doesn't need to honor the visitation schedule.

4. Fears: I'll never be loved. I'll be penniless. I can't handle the stress of the divorce. The kids will take his side. Mike's irresponsibility will damage the kids.

5. What I could have done differently in the past or do differently now? I could have confronted him when I first suspected his cheating and gotten out of the marriage sooner. I could have canceled the credit card, since it was in my name. I could have gone back to work when the kids went to kindergarten so I would be more financially self-sufficient. I could use coping skills, so I don't vent to the kids about Mike. I can't control whether or not Mike shows up to visit the kids as scheduled, but I could assure the kids it's not their fault when he doesn't.

Your list of resentments may be a lot longer than this example—pages, even. That's okay. Write as much as you want to about each person on your resentment list. Be sure to focus equally on your fears and your own behaviors: These are your *character defects,* the things you need to work on if you want to improve your life.

An important note: Be aware of your feelings as you do your inventory. It's normal to experience sadness and anger during this process, and you don't want to force yourself to write if you're numbing out, sobbing uncontrollably, or experiencing a cortisol dump from stress. Check in with yourself: "On a scale from 1–10, how high is my anxiety (or depression or rage)?" Aim for something in the 1–5 range.

If you're at an 8, 9, or 10, use one of the trauma resiliency exercises you learned in Chapter 11 to regulate your nervous system *before* returning to your inventory.

Don't feel pressured to do the divorce inventory all in one sitting. It may take a few days, weeks, or even months. You want it done right, not fast.

CHAPTER TWENTY

Cleaning House
Get Rid of Thoughts and Behaviors That Drag You Down

When you've completed your divorce inventory, make a separate list of your *fears* and *character defects.* You will probably notice that they repeat themselves. A note about the term *character defects:* Having defects does not make you defective. We all think and behave in unskillful ways from time to time. Getting healthy means that you put on your grown-up pants and change what needs to be changed.

Common divorce-related fears are:
- "I'll always be alone."
- "I'm unlovable."
- "I'll be financially destitute."

- "My kids will resent me."
- "I'll die from the stress."

Character defects that show up in situations involving resentment usually include thoughts and behavior based on:

- Contempt.
- Envy.
- Self-pity.
- Impatience.
- Self-righteousness.
- Pride.
- Vengefulness.
- Bitterness.
- Distrust.

Once you've completed your whole divorce inventory and identified your frequent character defects, you're going to do a fifth step on your divorce. I've modeled this process on the fifth step of twelve-step programs, which reads: *"We admitted to God, to ourselves, and to another human being the exact nature of our wrongs."* The step is to go and tell someone what's in your divorce inventory.

It can be helpful to find a mentor with whom you can share your inventory. If writing your inventory is taking longer than you'd expected, you might want to meet with your mentor in stages and share two or three resentments at a time. This person might be able to point out your blind spots when you're struggling.

Friends and relatives generally don't make great mentors because they're likely to hate your ex-spouse as much as you do. You're better off choosing a therapist, a clergyperson, a spiritual guide, or an all-around sage. Perhaps someone who worked hard to develop a good relationship with an ex, or someone who simply has a lot of life skills. A more objective person will help you keep the focus on personal accountability, not blame.

Whomever you choose, make sure that person isn't judgmental. The last thing you want to hear is: "I can't believe you were ever with that nutcase!"

Here's the plan once you have found a willing listener. Ask your mentor to meet you so you can "turn over" your inventory by reading it to them. Some people prefer to meet in a neutral zone like a park or a coffee shop instead of their homes. It might feel better to air your grievances elsewhere, as a symbolic gesture of clearing bad divorce juju from your personal space.

Usually, the turning-over process is accompanied by huge relief. You reveal the bad things that were done to you and you get compassion. You also admit things you did that were embarrassing or cause you shame and your mentor will often normalize the experience: "Oh, that's not so bad" or "I've done that too."

Turning over your inventory doesn't mean you'll develop warm, fuzzy feelings for your ex or never feel another twinge of resentment. But it's a kind of ritual to make peace with the past and commit to personal growth.

After doing your divorce inventory, you will be ready to commit to the ongoing work of addressing your character defects. This process will be like a twelve-step program's sixth step: *"We were entirely ready to have God remove all these defects of character."* Feelings such as fear, self-pity, and rage can be like barnacles on a ship's hull; they're surprisingly hard to get rid of because it's easy to dwell in them and feed them energy. As much as these unwanted visitors make you miserable, they're familiar. It can be easier wallowing in bitterness than practicing self-care, dating wisely, using time productively, or rebuilding a career.

A good way to work on releasing unwanted feelings (aka character defects) is to focus on them during your mindfulness practice. When you write down your intentions, you might say something like this:

- "I ask for the willingness to let go of self-pity, fear, and bitterness."
- "I'm making space to bring gratitude and abundance into my life."
- "I no longer let my ex determine my happiness."

You can turn the meditation part of your mindfulness practice into a sixth-step reflection. First, notice if any of your pesky character defects have shown up for an unwanted visit. Scan your body to see if there are corresponding physical sensations. Maybe your head is pounding. Instead of reacting to your headache with a thought like *What if I have a brain tumor?!,* simply observe it. Getting tense about your headache will probably make it worse. So, breathe deeply and do your best to soften into the experience.

Sit comfortably for a few moments, close your eyes, and follow your breath. Imagine putting all of your character defects into a bag and releasing them into a field. Watch them float away like butterflies in the wind. Notice how your body feels when you give yourself permission to let go of your unproductive thought patterns and unwanted feelings. Perhaps your headache is dissipating. Or your muscles feel more relaxed. Maybe breathing seems easier.

If fear and self-pity come back to visit you during your meditation, mentally acknowledge what's happening as it happens. For example: *There's fear. There's self-pity. This feels really hard.*

Don't judge or criticize yourself for having these feelings. Don't write off the meditation, your mindfulness practice, as being worthless. Breaking a habit—in this case, the habit of being afraid, resentful, and self-pitying—takes time. Developing new habits, like self-care and skillful responses to difficult events, will take time as well.

So, give yourself credit for actively committing to your personal growth. Reminding yourself of your intentions to think and act in healthy ways when you're feeling overwhelmed will help you focus your attention on the positive.

CHAPTER TWENTY-ONE

Writing a Personal Mission Statement

A personal mission statement is a formal summary of your values and goals. Getting clear about what's important to you is another important step in mastering the developmental task of divorce, which is shifting from blame to accountability.

Maybe you compromised your values during your marriage. Maybe you've acted in ways that go against your values since your divorce. Or maybe you've never really known what your values are.

Now is the time to figure them out.

"Winning" in divorce doesn't make people happy. If you have a vengeful spouse who's gotten the better end of the post-divorce deal, you know what I mean. Getting the house, all the stuff in the house, and the preferred child (or pet) custody schedule may make someone feel victorious for a while, but these things, by themselves, will not lead to contentment in the long run. They are external circumstances and hitching your happiness to externals is a lousy life strategy. If circumstances change, and they always do, happiness flies out the door.

The way to be content is to live in accordance with your values. When you know what's important to you and you make choices that reflect this, you are living in integrity. All the money, good looks, fame, and sexy partners in the world will never make you happy if you don't have integrity. If you don't have a good relationship with yourself, you will remain addicted to controlling people, places, and things in order to keep misery at bay. For example, compulsively writing your ex emails to make him change his personality, admit you're right, or gain his respect, is an attempt to control what he thinks so you can feel better. In order to heal, in twelve-step parlance, you need to stop giving your ex free rent in your head. This is what it means to disengage emotionally from your divorce.

Having a personal mission statement to guide your actions will help you live in integrity. Preparing this statement is a three-step process.

Step 1. Write a Values List

Grab your notebook and make a list of values that are important to you. Here are some examples of values to which people commonly ascribe.

- Honesty
- Commitment
- A strong work ethic
- Financial stability
- Compassion
- Trustworthiness
- Empathy
- Self-esteem
- Love
- Emotional availability
- Humor
- Service
- Responsibility
- Patience
- Self-care

Brainstorm. You may find that you think you've entirely finished your list and then, a week later, something else will occur to you. If it does, go back and write it down.

Step 2. Write a Goals List

After you've completed your values list, it's time to write down your goals. These might be:

- Increase my earnings.
- Be more patient.
- Learn effective communication strategies with my ex.
- Strengthen my mindfulness practice.
- Have better boundaries.
- Join a yoga studio.
- Cut ties, or minimize contact, with toxic people.
- Save for a trip to Europe with the kids.
- Write the book I've been meaning to write.
- Become more politically active.
- Decrease cell phone/social media/screen time.
- See friends more.
- Date trustworthy people.
- Accumulate six months' worth of savings.

Going forward, make sure your actions and goals line up with your values. For instance, if trustworthiness is a value and dating trustworthy people is a goal, yet you keep finding yourself drawn to charismatic, but dodgy people on dating apps, then you will know you're not living in alignment with your values.

The same thing goes for self-care. If you've set self-care as a value and goal, but you're routinely scarfing cookies, wallowing on the couch, avoiding exercise, and are "too busy" to fit in your mindfulness practice, then you will need to adjust your actions.

Step 3. Write a Personal Mission Statement

Once you have a solid idea of both your values and your goals, see if you can distill them into a single, concise mission statement.

Here are some mission statements from successful businesses and organizations.

- "Inspire and nurture the human spirit—one person, one cup, and one neighborhood at a time." —Starbucks
- "Create a better everyday life for many people." —Ikea
- "Improve the health and happiness of the world." —Headspace
- "Reconnect people through transportation and bring communities together." —Lyft
- "Spread ideas." —TED

And my own: "Use my experience and my words, both written and spoken, to empower people going through high-conflict divorce."

When I doubted my ability to write a book that was worth reading or when I was tempted to binge-watch the latest Netflix series instead of sitting down and beginning the often painful process of cobbling sentences together, I remembered my mission statement. Reflecting on my intention helped ground me. It got me to put aside my worries and excuses, and just focus on writing what I knew to be true, as simply as I could, with the occasional irreverent turn of phrase.

Now it's your turn. In your notebook jot down some personal or professional mission statements. Don't obsess about getting them perfect, just write down ideas as they come to mind. Play around. Then circle the one that feels most right.

Let your mission statement infuse your choices going forward. And whenever you get that niggling feeling that you might be doing the wrong thing, ask yourself: "Does this jive with my mission statement?" If the answer is any shade of no, don't do it!

CHAPTER TWENTY-TWO

Using Creativity and Humor to Heal

I t's okay—even recommended—to have fun on your personal growth journey. Numerous psychological studies have shown the healing power of both creativity and humor. While divorce may have robbed you of the things you loved, doing something creative allows you to make something new. Humor heals because it's almost impossible to feel dreary when you're laughing.

Be Creative

The act of being creative is a way to practice mindfulness. Writing, playing music, gardening, cooking, or any other activity that uses your imagination grounds you in the present. When you're focused on making something in real time, it's hard to worry about the future or ruminate about the past.

Being creative also can help you work through painful feelings. It's kind of like art therapy. Sometimes it's easier to process emotions nonverbally.

It's exciting to watch something interesting and beautiful emerge from your mind. You'll feel good about yourself, and think, *Look, I did this cool thing!* And you'll have gotten a welcome respite from obsessing about your ex.

Cultivate a Sense of Humor

One of my mother's favorite sayings when I was a kid was, "You can't get through life without a sense of humor." Was she ever right! Especially in the case of divorce. Slogging through your days cataloging all your grievances and worrying about the next bomb your ex is going to drop on your head does you absolutely no good. That is, after all, the reason you're reading this book. Presumably, you're sick of feeling sick and tired of letting divorce run the show.

I'll be blunt: If you don't have a sense of humor, you need to get one. Studies have shown that just smiling can change your brain chemistry and lower blood pressure. So do things that make you smile, or better yet, laugh. Watch comedy specials on

Netflix, read a humor book, or just hang out with friends that crack you up.

The late Nora Ephron, well-known author and screenwriter, penned a ragingly funny novel called *Heartburn,* published in 1983. It was based on her marriage to (and divorce from) her second husband, famed journalist Carl Bernstein, who left her for his mistress when she was pregnant.

The book focuses on how the main character, Rachel, pulls herself together: through humor and creativity. A cookbook writer, Rachel chops, bakes, and sautés her way through her divorce. Interspersed between chapters chronicling her life and the end of her marriage are recipes.

Heartburn went on to become a movie starring Meryl Streep. And in 2010, Ephron developed *Huffington Post: Divorce* with its darkly humorous tagline: "Marriages come and go, but divorce is forever."

I loved Nora Ephron—from afar. If she had not shared her trademark dark humor and creativity with the world then I might never have cultivated my own creativity, written my first article, and found my niche as a psychotherapist specializing in counseling people going through high-conflict divorces.

Healing Yourself Benefits Others

The article I wrote for *Huffington Post* in 2013, "What Therapists Don't Tell You about Divorcing a High-conflict Personality," gave me national exposure as a divorce expert, both as a therapist and a writer. I wrote for *Huffington Post* until the website closed its contributor platform in 2018, and also parlayed my writing credits there into other writing gigs that helped supplement my post-divorce income. Years of honing my craft ultimately gave me the confidence to write this book.

So, think about that whenever you feel your divorce is beating you. There's a way out: through learning about high-conflict divorce strategies, taking accountability for your own behaviors, and living with intention with some humor and creativity sprinkled in.

Your healing process doesn't just help you, it impacts those around you, producing ripple effects that are felt through all your communities, and to a varying degree, with the wider world. Healing yourself connects you to your higher purpose, to something greater than yourself.

I was like you once. Divorce shame defined me. I felt like Hester Prynne in *The Scarlet Letter,* but with a red "D" on my forehead. It took me years to figure out my part in the mess in which I found myself, and to stop giving all my power away. They were profoundly painful years. I wouldn't have chosen them, and yet I'm grateful for them, because they forced me to grow up—into a better person, and a better professional.

I wrote this book to help others get better faster. I can't tell you how long your healing will take, but I know that following the guidelines I've laid out on these pages will teach you how to transcend your high-conflict divorce and grow up in the process.

I'll close now with another quote from Nora Ephron, the same quote that began this book. It bears repeating.

"For a long time, divorce was the most important thing about me. Now it's not."[1]

END NOTES

Introduction
1. Nora Ephron. *I Remember Nothing: And Other Reflections* (New York: Knopf, 2010), p. 126.

Chapter 2: Personality Disorders
1. George K. Simon. *In Sheep's Clothing: Understanding and Dealing with Manipulative People* (Marion, MI.: Parkhurst Brothers Press, 2010), page 133.
2. Ibid, pp. 79–80, 95.

Chapter 6: High-conflict Divorce Is Addictive
1. "Public Policy Statement: Short Definition of Addiction," American Society of Addiction Medicine (August 15, 2011), https://www.asam.org/docs/default-source/public-policy-statements/1definition_of_addiction_short_4-11.pdf?sfvrsn=6e36cc2_0.

Chapter 10: Understanding the Online Disinhibition Effect

1. John Suler. "The Online Disinhibition Effect," *Cyberpsychology and Behavior*, vol. 7, no. 3, pp. 321–26.

Chapter 11: Managing the Trauma of Your Divorce

1. "How to Recognize High Cortisol Symptoms," *University Health News* (February 7, 2019), https://universityhealthnews.com/daily/depression/how-to-recognize-high-cortisol-symptoms.
2. Ibid.
3. Ibid.
4. Kevin M. Gilmartin. "The Brotherhood of Biochemistry: Its Implications for a Police Career," *Understanding Human Behavior for Effective Police Work, third edition,* edited by H.E. Russell and A. Beigel (New York, N.Y.: Basic Books, 1990), http://emotionalsurvival.com/brotherhood_of_biochemistry.htm.
5. Ibid.
6. Kevin Gilmartin. "Psychological Resiliency: Keeping Good People Good," *Police News* (September 2014), pp. 17–21.
7. Kevin M. Gilmartin. "Lethal Triad: Keys to Emotional Survival," *Police News* (October 2014), pp. 16–17.
8. Ibid, p. 17.

Final Thoughts

Nora Ephron. *I Remember Nothing: And Other Reflections* (New York: Knopf, 2010), p. 126.

Books

Bill Eddy. *BIFF: Quick Responses to High-conflict People, Their Personal Attacks, Hostile Email and Social Media Meltdowns* (San Diego, CA.: High Conflict Institute Press, 2011).

Bill Eddy. *It's All Your Fault! 12 Tips for Managing People Who Blame Others for Everything* (San Diego, CA.: High Conflict Institute Press, 2012).

Bill Eddy and Randi Kreger. *Splitting: Protecting Yourself While Divorcing Someone with Borderline or Narcissistic Personality Disorder* (Oakland, CA.: New Harbinger Publications, 2011).

John Bowlby. *A Secure Base: Parent-Child Attachment and Healthy Human Development* (New York, N.Y.: Basic Books, 1988).

Nora Ephron. *Heartburn* (New York: Alfred A. Knopf, 1983).

Anne Lamott. *Almost Everything: Notes on Hope* (New York, N.Y.: Riverhead, 2018).

Amir Levine and Rachel Heller. *Attached: The New Science of Adult Attachment and How It Can Help You Find—and Keep—Love* (New York, N.Y.: TarcherPerigee, 2010).

Phillip Moffit *Emotional Chaos to Clarity: Move from the Chaos of the Reactive Mind to the Clarity of the Responsive Mind* (New York, N.Y.: Hudson Street Press, 2012)

George K. Simon. *In Sheep's Clothing: Understanding and Dealing with Manipulative People* (Marion, MI.: Parkhurst Brothers Press, 2010).

Tina Swithin. *Divorcing a Narcissist: Advice from the Battlefield* (San Luis Obispo, CA.: Tina Swithin, 2014).

Articles

"Public Policy Statement: Short Definition of Addiction," American Society of Addiction Medicine (August 15, 2011), https://www.asam.org/docs/default-source/ public-policy-statements/1definition_of_ addiction_short_4-11.pdf?sfvrsn=6e36cc2_0.

"Erikson's Stages of Psychosocial Development," Wikipedia (accessed February 27, 2019), https://en.wikipedia.org/wiki/Erikson%27s_stage s_of_psychosocial_development.

"How to Recognize High Cortisol Symptoms," *University Health News* (February 7, 2019), https://universityhealthnews.com/daily/depressi on/ how-to-recognize-high-cortisol-symptoms.

Kevin Gilmartin. "The Brotherhood of Biochemistry: Its Implications for a Police Career,"

Understanding Human Behavior for Effective Police Work, third edition, edited by H.E. Russell and A. Beigel (New York: Basic Books, 1990).

Kevin Gilmartin. "Lethal Triad: Keys to Emotional Survival," *Police News* (October 2014), pp. 16–17.

Kevin Gilmartin. "Psychological Resiliency: Keeping Good People Good," *Police News* (September 2014), pp. 17–21.

C.M. Hearing, et al. "Physical Exercise for Treatment of Mood Disorders: A Critical Review," Current Behavioral Neuroscience Reports, vol. 3, no. 4 (December 2016), pp. 350–59.

Kati Morton. "What is Somatic Experiencing in Trauma Therapy?" YouTube (January 30, 2017), https://www.youtube.com/watch?v=aDYRkLAAH2U.

John Suler. "The Online Disinhibition Effect," *Cyberpsychology and Behavior,* vol. 7, no. 3, pp. 321–26.

ACKNOWLEDGMENTS

This book would not exist if it were not for the contributions many individuals have made to my life and writing career. I am grateful to my mother, who put a little black journal in my seven-year-old hands and told me to write my stories in it.

To my sister, Allison, who has read just about everything I've ever written, and who has been my biggest cheerleader.

To the editors of *Huffington Post: Divorce,* who published my first work on high-conflict divorce.

To the late Nora Ephron, who came up with the idea for *Huffington Post: Divorce,* and without whom this book might not have been written.

To Bill Eddy of the High Conflict Institute, whose books and wisdom have informed my therapy practice and my writing about divorce.

To my friend and colleague Scott Musgrove, who told me to just start the damn book already, and who shared his considerable expertise and insight during the outline and early draft stages.

To my editor, Stephanie Gunning, for her enthusiasm, incisiveness, and commitment to excellence. She helped me clarify what was vague.

To my children, Jack and Kat, who motivated me to transcend my own high-conflict divorce.

And to my ex-husband, who taught me what I needed to know.

For Additional Support

To read my blog and sign up for my online newsletter, visit my website:

VirginiaGilbertMFT.com

Request a Free 15-minute Consultation

(323) 528-6747

Hire Me to Speak to Your Organization

VirginiaGilbertMFT.com/contact

Connect with Me Via the Social Networks

Twitter.com/vgilbertmft

Instagram.com/vgilbertmft

LinkedIn.com/in/virginia-gilbert-lmft-208b0b3

Facebook.com/VirginiaGilbertLMFT

Pinterest.com/vgilbertmft

Recommended Organizations

Breathwork for Recovery
BreathworkforRecovery.com

The EMDR Institute
EMDR.com

The High Conflict Institute
HighConflictInstitute.com

ABOUT THE AUTHOR

Virginia Gilbert, MFT, is a psychotherapist and writer based in Los Angeles, California. Some of her written work has appeared in *Huffington Post, Good Men Project, Addiction.com, Covey Club,* and Weinberger Law Group. *Transcending High-conflict Divorce* is her first book.

Made in the USA
Middletown, DE
04 March 2020